Ambush at Central Park

AMBUSH AT CENTRAL PARK

When the IRA Came to New York

Mark Bulik

EMPIRE STATE EDITIONS

AN IMPRINT OF FORDHAM UNIVERSITY PRESS

NEW YORK   2023

Fordham University Press has no responsibility for the persistence or accuracy of URLs for external or third-party Internet websites referred to in this publication and does not guarantee that any content on such websites is, or will remain, accurate or appropriate.

Fordham University Press also publishes its books in a variety of electronic formats. Some content that appears in print may not be available in electronic books.

Visit us online at www.fordhampress.com/empire-state-editions.

Library of Congress Cataloging-in-Publication Data

Names: Bulik, Mark, author.
Title: Ambush at Central Park : when the IRA came to New York / Mark Bulik.

Description: First edition. | New York : Empire State Editions, an imprint
   of Fordham University Press, 2023. | Includes bibliographical references
   and index.
Identifiers: LCCN 2022057242 | ISBN 9781531502607 (hardback) | ISBN
   9781531502607 (epub)
Subjects: LCSH: Terrorism—New York (State)—New York—History—20th
   century. | Irish Republican Army. | O'Connor, Cruxy, 1893–
Classification: LCC HV6432.5.I75 B85 2023 | DDC
   363.32509747/10905—dc23/eng/20221206
LC record available at https://lccn.loc.gov/2022057242

Printed in the United States of America

25 24 23   5 4 3 2 1

First edition

Dedicated to my wife,
Barbara Hennessy

CONTENTS

Photographs follow page 86

Ambush at Central Park

Bloody Anniversaries

"THERE IS A significance in dates," the president declared.[1]

Warren G. Harding was addressing a top-hat crowd—the American secretary of state, the Venezuelan foreign minister, assorted South American ambassadors, the governor of New York, the mayor of New York City, and sundry diplomats and dignitaries. Behind them stood a crowd of up to twenty thousand,[2] gathered at the highest point in Central Park to hear the newly inaugurated president—he'd taken office just the month before.

The dignitaries had removed their top hats when the president arrived. But April 19, 1921, was raw and wet, and Harding had tried to drop a hint, saying they might all get a cold. When that didn't work—they all still just sat there, hats in their laps—Harding looked around, laughed, and put on his.

They all followed suit, and he launched into his speech.

"This is the anniversary of the Battle of Lexington, when the colonies of North America made their first sacrifice in blood for independence and new standards of freedom," Harding intoned. "On this same day, a generation later, Venezuela's struggle for freedom had its immortal beginning."

Then he gave a ringing affirmation of the Monroe Doctrine, saying the United States would fight, if necessary, to keep the Americas from "the colonial enterprises of Old World powers."[3] But before all of Harding's saber-rattling and speechifying about blood sacrifice, two young sisters briefly stole the show.

Their hands trembling, their hair ribboned in the red, blue, and yellow of the Venezuelan flag, nine-year-old Mariquita and her five-year-old sister,

Patricia, gripped cords attached to some bunting. The bunting covered a statue so large that it frightened them as they shivered in the cold drizzle. Patricia, a perfectionist even at age five, seemed nervous to the point of tears. Standing by for moral support were their mother and the sculptor who had created the giant statue, Sally James Farnham. In a large veiled black hat, Mrs. Farnham seemed to the girls as formidable as her creation— they couldn't imagine how she had managed to get the huge figure of the man up on that immense horse.

Then came the command, and the girls pulled the cords attached to the giant American and Venezuelan flag bunting that covered the statue. Everything went fine for Mariquita, but Patricia's cord caught on the prancing steed. A sailor from the honor guard came to her rescue, grasping her hand and pulling. Down came the bunting.

The crowd roared. There in full caped glory rode Simon Bolivar, the great hero of South American independence, astride an immense charger.

On the way back to their seats, the girls stopped to present gifts to President Harding and the Venezuelan foreign minister, Dr. E. Gil-Borges: two stick pins, made from the gold buttons of Bolivar's uniform. They'd been passed down to the girls' mother, Catalina Violante Páez, the granddaughter of the first president of Venezuela, General José Antonio Páez, who had fought beside Bolivar to free Venezuela from the Spanish crown.

Then Harding stepped forward to speak about inter-American relations and the significance of dates and blood sacrifice in the cause of independence from colonial powers.

When all was said and done and the president and Mrs. Harding had made their way to his open touring car, nine-year-old Mariquita wriggled her way through the crowd, clawed her way onto the running board and gave the president a personal farewell.

"I just came to say goodbye, Mr. Harding," she said.

The president tipped his top hat, the first lady offered a sweet smile, and off they went as a marine lifted Mariquita to the ground.

The crowd was dissipating—the photographers taking a few last shots, and the reporters tucking away their notebooks. The event would lead the next day's front pages, with the city newspapers hammering home Harding's tough stand against European imperialism.

"U.S. WILL UPHOLD MONROE DOCTRINE EVEN IF IT MEANS WAR," blared the *New York Herald*.

War headlines could always be counted on to convince the undecided to cough up a couple of pennies for the paper, and the anticolonial angle had a special resonance in this particular town, at this particular time.

Ireland's war for independence from Britain was reaching a fever pitch in the first half of 1921, and New York City had more Irish than Dublin.[4] At least 630,000 Gotham residents were first- or second-generation Irish Americans, many with parents, siblings, aunts, uncles, and cousins back in the old country, giving them an immediate stake in the fighting there. Hundreds of thousands more city residents came from older Irish stock, but if their family links to the old sod were more distant, in many cases the emotional ties were strong, nonetheless.

The Irish dominated the Catholic Church, the police department, and Democratic politics in the city; their clout on the docks was such that in 1920 longshoremen staged a political strike in support of Irish independence by refusing to handle British ships.

That same year New Yorkers raised a million dollars to aid the fight for Irish independence, thanks to the barnstorming of the leading spokesman for the anticolonial cause, Eamon de Valera, himself a son of New York City. His tour of the United States had left Irish American supporters of independence divided, but it created invaluable publicity for the struggle at home.

He certainly impressed Mariquita and Patricia's father, the Irish writer and nationalist Seumas MacManus, who described de Valera as "Cool, resolved, gentle, masterly, humble, firm."[5]

MacManus's anticolonial credentials were almost as strong and certainly more recent than those of General Páez. Nearly twenty years before, Mac-Manus had been part of a small group that, in his own words, "formed the nucleus of Sinn Fein,"[6] the Irish movement battling for independence even as Harding's words about Lexington hung in the air near 83rd and Central Park West.

He recalled years later that he had to quit a teaching position in County Donegal, after he was wrongly suspected of being that most hated figure in Ireland—an informer. "Things became so hot for me that I had to resign my position," he wrote.[7]

Eventually MacManus landed on New York's Upper West Side, where he kept involved with the fight for Irish independence.

And that fight came to the sidewalks of the Upper West Side, practically in the shadow of the Bolivar statue, a year to the week after the MacManus girls unveiled the monument. On April 13, 1922, a team of gunmen from the Irish Republican Army ambushed a former comrade who had betrayed the independence movement and fled to New York.

Just before the shooting, the gunmen shooed away some children loitering near the Bolivar statue. They didn't want any kids getting caught in a crossfire.

The location of the ambush may or may not have been a coincidence, but the timing was certainly no accident. The informer was shot a year after he got six IRA comrades killed by crown forces. That massacre in Ballycannon, Cork, came on the Wednesday of Holy Week, known in Ireland as "Spy Wednesday," for the day Judas betrayed Jesus for thirty pieces of silver. The Cork informer was a paid spy, too, and he was gunned down in New York on April 13, 1922—Holy Thursday.

"Almost a year exactly since the Ballycannon murders," the triggerman said.[8]

As Harding put it, there is a significance in dates.

What follows is the story of four comrades from the Irish War for Independence, and their paths to and from a bullet-riddled reunion in Manhattan. It is the story of the war's main battleground, Cork, and New York's role in the struggle. It is a tale of gunmen and gunrunners, informers and spies, courage and betrayal, assassinations and abductions.

It is the story of the only authorized attack by the Irish Republican Army on American soil.

Chapter 1

The Ambush

WHEN THE RELENTLESS avengers of the Irish Republican Army finally caught up with Cruxy O'Connor in Manhattan that fine spring evening, they sent six bullets his way—one for each man the informer had sent to an early grave the year before.

Four of the gunshots found their target, and as a cop reached the crumpled victim on the steps of a finishing school at 84th and Central Park West, O'Connor was clutching a revolver with a spent shell in each chamber. After one of his attackers dropped the gun, the fallen O'Connor apparently had grabbed it, intending to defend himself.[1] But the weapon was useless by then—his assailant had emptied the revolver at him.

O'Connor hadn't had much luck in the weapons department lately.

There was that machine gun they had given him for the ambush the year before—when he told them that it jammed just as the shooting started, the boys started looking at him funny. Not long after that, he'd made the mistake of taking a pistol to Sunday Mass. The coppers threw a cordon around the church, and oh dear God, what a massacre that led to. Six men dead, including Willie Deasy, his next-door neighbor, just twenty years old.

Pa Murray and the boys blamed him. They had stalked O'Connor through three countries—he'd barely escaped with his life when they tried to poison him. And he'd had to quit his job as a bookkeeper at the B. Altman department store a month earlier, after the gunmen had started haunting his workplace.

For weeks now, his only escape from the cramped apartment on the Upper West Side of Manhattan had been a walk and a smoke. He varied his route, just to be on the safe side.[2] But there were some evenings, like this one, when he couldn't stay cooped up in the flat on Columbus Avenue with his parents, his brother, his sister-in-law, and their toddler. The warm spring evening beckoned, its soft westerly breezes stirring the curtains of Manhattan. He needed a cigarette. He needed a stroll.

It was a few minutes to eight o'clock on the evening of April 13, 1922. O'Connor came bounding down the stairs of his apartment building, but even as he headed out the door, he knew, on some level, that this was crazy. Three of County Cork's deadliest gunmen—Murray, Danny Healy, and Martin Donovan—were out there somewhere in the New York night, just itching to take a shot. There'd be hell to pay for what he'd done, and the devil's own bill collectors wanted their due.

O'Connor headed east up 83rd Street, toward Central Park, where the sheer black rock of Bolivar Hill loomed like a dungeon wall. When he reached Central Park West, he turned north on the west side of the street.

The temperature was in the low 60s, so there were plenty of other pedestrians out taking the night air. O'Connor smoked nervously, his eyes on their faces. When he reached 84th Street, he glanced to the left, and sweet Jesus, there was Pa Murray himself, with another guy, headed straight for him.

O'Connor dashed across the street to the wall that lines Central Park, glancing back at Murray and puffing furiously on a cigarette. He headed north, then suddenly reversed himself, and that's when Danny Healy came out from behind a tree right smack in front of him. In a gray coat and gray fedora, Healy looked like some kind of natty avenging angel.

It all happened so fast. Healy, pointing a revolver at his chest, saying something like "I've got you now."[3]

Then pulling the trigger.

Danny Healy and Martin Donovan had been near the corner of 83rd and Columbus, staking out the flat, when O'Connor walked out the door and headed toward the park. Pa Murray and Mullins, a guy from Derry who signed on for the hunt, were a little further up Columbus, near 84th Street.

Healy asked Donovan to tell Murray and Mullins to head up 84th Street toward the park, where they might be able to head off O'Connor, while Healy came up from behind him. Once he caught sight of Murray, O'Connor had been too preoccupied to notice Healy until he stepped out from behind the tree.

The gunman thought his first bullet caught O'Connor in the chest, but he dashed across Central Park West into the 84th Street intersection. Healy chased him, blazing away, hitting O'Connor twice. To Healy's astonishment, O'Connor kept going, ducking around a trolley.

Healy followed, firing a shot that thudded into a building. Four bullets gone, only two left, and his prey was still scrambling.

O'Connor kept changing direction, like a panicked hare flushed by a pack of hounds. He tried to go north on the west side of Central Park West, but almost ran into Donovan, who pointed a revolver and squeezed the trigger.

Nothing—a misfire.

But the bullets were finally having an effect on O'Connor's adrenaline-infused body. Wounded, winded, and bleeding, he slumped to the sidewalk.

"I caught up with him and fired twice more at him, hitting him," Healy recalled.

As Healy blasted away, the getaway car came roaring up to the intersection, a kid from the Bronx at the wheel. Healy knew he was supposed to get in, but he just stood there, frozen, surrounded by a large group of gaping pedestrians. He couldn't imagine he was going to get away with it. This wasn't home, where people knew to look away when Murray and the boys cut someone down in the street. This was the very heart of Manhattan—and a horde of people were staring straight at him.

One thought kept going through his head: "No chance of escape."

Then Donovan's commanding voice rang out: "Run for it, Danny. Run!"

Christ, but Healy took him literally. Donovan saw Healy snap out of it, but instead of getting in the car, Healy walked casually for a bit, then broke into a run west on 84th Street. And Donovan saw the crowd of stunned pedestrians form into a posse that quickly gave chase. Dozens of them. They figured it was an underworld hit, and they weren't about to let a bunch of gangsters get away with murder in the middle of Manhattan.[4]

Donovan climbed into the car. It looked natural enough—he was wearing a chauffeur's coat he'd gotten from the Bronx kid's family. And then they were all giving chase, the car and the crowd, until the car got ahead of the posse and kept pace with Healy for a bit while they tried to talk him into getting in so they could all get the hell out of there.

The trouble they went through to get that getaway car—"Over 1,000 cars in the St. Patrick's Day Parade," and they couldn't use one of them, Donovan complained.[5] Finally Johnny Culhane from the Bronx came through—he had an auto rental and taxi business—but he wanted no part of driving a getaway car for a killing. Culhane was already facing a boatload of legal trouble involving several hundred Ireland-bound tommy guns the feds had confiscated from a rust bucket docked in Hoboken. As Culhane begged off, his seventeen-year-old son James jumped in, exasperated.

"I'll drive the damn car," he said.[6]

Which was how they ended up with a kid from the Bronx as wheelman. And now, after all that, Healy wouldn't get in the car.

Even with half of Manhattan on his tail.

Clearly, someone would have to put a stop to this posse business, Donovan realized. At 34, he was the grownup in the group, older than the others by a decade. He'd have to do it, or it wouldn't get done.

It would have helped if he'd still had the revolver, but Donovan had tossed it after it misfired—why keep a useless, incriminating weapon at a crime scene? So now he'd have to pull off a bluff—one man against close to fifty. But Donovan had gotten Danny Healy into this mess by recruiting him for the O'Connor job. Healy hadn't hesitated then. Donovan didn't now.

He got out of the car and confronted the crowd, just fifteen feet away. If even one of them dared to make a quick lunge, he'd be hopelessly overpowered in seconds. So Donovan slid a hand into his coat pocket, as if to pull a gun.

"What do you want—trouble?" he asked the man at the front.[7]

"No."

"Well, where are you going?"

"I'm going right back to where I came from." The man turned on his heels and did just that, followed by most of the crowd.

Then another quick conversation with Danny about getting in the car, but it didn't do any good. The normally reliable Healy was rattled, out of his element, not thinking straight. Donovan had shouted "run," so run he would. Healy and O'Connor, the shooter and the shot, had one thing in common that fine spring evening—they were bound and determined to stretch their legs.

Even if it killed them.

As the getaway car pulled away, Healy continued on foot, passing the building where O'Connor lived, 483 Columbus Avenue. But he wasn't alone.

A single pursuer remained on his tail.

Healy zigzagged his way through the street grid of the Upper West Side toward the subway entrance at 79th and Broadway, unable to shake the man tracking him. He caught a bit of luck inside the station—a train was just about to leave as he entered. He jumped in as the doors closed, leaving his pursuer behind.

Healy got off at 42nd Street, emerging into the bright lights and swirling human tides of Times Square. "Crowded at night," he noted. He headed south, to the rendezvous point—Jimmy McGee's apartment on the East Side near 38th Street.[8] Jimmy was a big shot in the marine engineers' union and served as a dockside fixer for the boys. On this job, he had fixed them up with revolvers, including the one that misfired for Martin Donovan.

After a long time, Pa Murray showed up at McGee's place. But Donovan was still out on the street, and they were starting to worry. Had he gone back to the Bronx with their teenage driver? Had someone from the crowd that Martin turned back decided to come after him?

Finally, Donovan arrived. No, he told them, nobody had interfered with him after that show of bravado on 84th Street. That was the thing about Martin—the man could radiate cool menace with a look and a word. He'd make you think he was reaching for a gun, even if all he had in his pocket was lint.

Back at the scene of the shooting, onlookers lifted the gravely wounded victim to the steps of Semple School for Girls, a finishing school. O'Connor, 26, had been shot in the back, the side, the stomach, and the jaw.

A patrolman walking his beat on Central Park West just south of 81st Street heard the shots and came running. As Officer Jansen hurried to O'Connor, he saw the bleeding man clutching a revolver. When the officer examined it, he found the six spent shells. He asked O'Connor who he was and where he lived, and the victim told him.

But when Jansen asked, "Whose gun is this?" O'Connor didn't answer—he had lapsed into unconsciousness.[9]

At that point, a woman who had witnessed the whole thing spoke up.

"That man didn't do any shooting," she said of O'Connor.

The victim was rushed off to the Reconstruction Hospital at 100th and Central Park West, where doctors didn't like his odds. Then the detectives took over. In the immediate aftermath, they considered various theories about the shooting—that it had something to do with bootlegging, or a quarrel about a girl.

The truth, they soon discovered, was far more complicated. One of O'Connor's relatives showed up at the scene and told the police that he had fled war-ravaged County Cork just the previous year. And that he had served in the Irish Republican Army, which was locked in a brutal war for independence from Britain. And that he "had been forced to leave Ireland because of threats of death that had been conveyed to him through mysterious channels."[10]

All of which added up to one astonishing conclusion: The Irish Republican Army had just conducted an attack on American soil.

The newspapers splashed the thing the next day.

"LINK SHOOTING HERE WITH IRISH WARFARE," the *New York Times* declared on the front page.

"SHOOTING VICTIM IN IRISH TREASON PLOT, SAY POLICE," the *Evening World* blared.

The *Times* story made clear that O'Connor knew the man who shot him, and knew he was being stalked. The *World* added that a fully loaded .38 Colt revolver had been recovered near 3 West 84th Street—witnesses had spotted a man running from the scene tossing something there. If the gun was fully loaded, it wasn't Healy's; he had emptied his. Pa Murray held on to his piece, so it had to be Donovan's. That was why none of the witnesses saw him draw a gun when he confronted the posse.

The newspapers offered eyewitness accounts from some young boys—the stories were contradictory in their details but consistent in their general thrust. The gunmen had warned the kids to clear out just before the shooting.

According to the *Times*, the boys were hanging out by the 83rd Street entrance to the park, just opposite the Bolivar statue, when a car pulled up. A man in a cap jumped out, told them he was a detective and asked what they were doing.

"We're just getting the air," one of the boys replied.

"Well, beat it on out of this part of the park, and get the air somewhere else," he replied.

In the *World*'s version, the boys were near the 85th Street entrance when they saw O'Connor and another man, talking in vehement tones as they headed out of the park. When the man with O'Connor spotted the boys, he demanded to know what they were doing.

Just playing, they said, whereupon he announced "I'm a detective. You'd better go play somewhere else. Get out of the park."

According to the *World*, the two men exited the park, talking loudly, and turned south on Central Park West. The victim broke into a run, and the other man pursued, blazing away.

The two stories don't fully jibe. In one, the "detective" is a guy in a cap who jumps out of a car; in the other he's the gunman, who we know was wearing a fedora, and instead of jumping out of a car he's strolling and talking with his intended target. Healy never said anything about warning away children. All we can be reasonably sure about is that one of the hit team chased away the boys, and Healy said something to O'Connor before shooting him.

It may have been the notion that he had a walk in the park and a lengthy conversation with O'Connor that caused Healy to scoff at some of the reporting.

"Needless to remark, the newspapers, the next day, carried reports of the shooting, some of which were highly colored," he said.

The papers played up the gray fedora so much that it was decided that Healy should ditch it. The next day Healy and Donovan deemed it advisable to quit the city and state of New York, leaving their digs on Lexington Avenue and beating it across the Hudson to stay with Donovan's sister in Jersey City.

The newspapers, meanwhile, had firmed up the Irish angle, reporting that investigators learned the victim had been condemned to death for passing information to the British that led to the killing of several IRA men.

An April 15 headline in the *Times* reported that O'Connor had been "SHOT AS A TRAITOR TO SINN FEIN ARMY."

On a visit to the hospital, O'Connor's mother let slip something that lent some credibility to the talk about him being an informer. Before joining the IRA, she said, he'd been a member of the Royal Irish Constabulary.[11]

There was one odd thing about the policeman/informer story, though: O'Connor, fading in and out of consciousness, absolutely refused to give the detectives any information about who had shot him, and why. He told them how it happened, but whenever he was asked to name his attackers, he would resolutely shake his head.

The informer wouldn't inform.

Chapter 2

***

Feuds and Fights

FOR A HUNDRED years, they've told stories in County Cork about Cruxy O'Connor, or "Connors the spy."[1] About a man torn by divided loyalties, in a nation riven by revolution, in a world ripped apart by war. About a normal lad from a normal Irish family from a normal Irish neighborhood who went off to join the British Army in World War I and rose to sergeant major. And how he became a hero in the horror of the trenches in France, earning his nickname when he was decorated for valor with the Croix de Guerre.

About how he returned home to Cork just as Ireland's struggle for independence from Britain was erupting and agreed to become a paid spy for the crown. About how he joined the Irish Republican Army and sabotaged the rebels during a crucial battle with British forces, claiming that his machine gun jammed. About how he got a beating afterward.

About how he betrayed six rebels from his Cork neighborhood, leading the police to their safe house and watching as they were captured, murdered, and mutilated. And how a vengeful IRA came within minutes of poisoning him in a British barracks in Cork, where he was being held for his protection, with a strychnine-laced meal delivered by a woman masquerading as his mother.

About how he fled for his life, first to London, and then to New York, pursued the whole way by the IRA. About how the avengers spotted him at the St. Patrick's Day parade, and killed him in a spectacular Manhattan ambush, with a gun borrowed from an Irish American cop. And how the

13

gunmen got away with it because an Irish American prosecutor sympathetic to the IRA quashed the case.

It's an incredible story. And the most incredible part is how much of it is actually true.

What we do know is this: Cruxy's real name was Patrick (Paddy to his friends), and he came from a quiet, respectable family. At least, that's what people usually said whenever the O'Connors landed in court after one of their many brawls, feuds, or run-ins with neighbors.

The O'Connors may or may not have been quiet and respectable, but they were certainly never ones to leave a blow unanswered—either with a back of the hand or a court summons.

The family—often called Connors or Conners—lived in a simple laborer's cottage at Mount Desert, a hillside on the western outskirts of Cork city with a fine view of the River Lee. The head of the family, John O'Connor, worked as an engine driver for the city.[2] He and his wife, the former Hannah Field, had four sons—John Jr., Jeremiah, Patrick, and Michael.

Patrick came into the world on February 15, 1893, the day after nationalist Irish politicians signaled their approval for a Home Rule bill that would have granted Ireland its first real measure of self-government since 1800.[3]

Divisions over Home Rule would tear at Ireland for the next three decades, and eventually land Patrick a punch to the jaw. Such brawls were not uncommon for the O'Connors, and quite often their sparring partners were their next-door neighbors, the Deasys, who lived fifty yards away.

Exactly when the feud first flared is uncertain, but the fire was raging by the end of the nineteenth century. In the spring of 1895, Cruxy's maternal grandfather, John Field, charged the head of the Deasy clan, William, with trying to break into the O'Connor home. Cruxy's mother, Hannah O'Connor, weighed in, accusing Deasy of threatening her with abusive language. Deasy was bound to the peace for twelve months and had to post twenty pounds as a surety.[4]

The peace was not assured for terribly long. Four years later, in June of 1899, William Deasy was back in the petty sessions, charged by John O'Connor with using abusive and threatening language against him. Deasy denied the accusation and spoke of a family dispute, with the wives filing charges and countercharges.[5] Again he had to put up bail to assure he would keep the peace.

But no matter how much bail piled up, it couldn't bury the feud, which moved from threats to physical violence in the new century.

In early November 1908, William Deasy swore out an assault summons for John O'Connor, saying that as he was passing the O'Connor home, John slammed him over the head with a blunt instrument and verbally abused him. O'Connor replied that the blunt instrument was the flat of his hand.

Meanwhile, Hannah O'Connor, took out a summons on Deasy's wife, Mary, saying she threw stones at her home.

O'Connor's attorney, William Dorgan, told the court his clients were respectable people, and that John was a sober, industrious man whose "life was made a misery and a burden" by the state of terror he was in from the Deasys.[6] He'd already been to court to have Deasy bound to the peace. The judge fined O'Connor for striking Deasy, bound both men to the peace for a year and discouraged further litigation, saying it "would only continue the squabbling."

And yet, for all the feuding, the two families were neighbors, in a world where neighbors needed to depend on each other, so at times they worked together and played together. In 1899, just a few months before the O'Connors and Deasys were squabbling in a Blarney court, the two wives were desperately trying to save the life of a child.

In early March of that year, Mary Deasy brought her children up to bed, carrying a lit candle. Her young daughter, Eliza, followed. Mary put the candle on a table, then left to attend to something in the yard. The next thing she knew, little Eliza was in flames. In the chaos that followed, Hannah O'Connor rushed over to help, rubbing oil onto Eliza's charred skin. Then she helped move the girl to the hospital. None of it did any good; Eliza died the next day.[7]

The O'Connors didn't confine their battles to the Deasys. There were also political fistfights, and fresh skirmishes in Ireland's age-old war between the gentry and the cottage dwellers.

In 1903, three of the O'Connor boys—John Jr., Jeremiah, and Patrick—tangled with a wealthy neighbor and leading member of the gentry, Robert Dunscombe, whose Mount Desert estate gave the neighborhood its name. The Dunscombes displayed some captured rebel weapons from the failed insurrection of 1798 at the gates of their estate as a warning to the locals, but the O'Connor siblings didn't get the message, or didn't care.[8] Dunscombe had the boys, who ranged in age from about sixteen to ten, charged with trespass, saying they frequently entered the grounds and threw stones. And his steward, Timothy O'Driscoll, raised the stakes by accusing John Jr. of threatening him with a knife.

The O'Connors' lawyer told the court that, sure, the boys trespassed, but they were quiet, respectable people, and that, by the way, O'Driscoll had tortured John Jr. by dragging him through a briar.[9] And what was all this nonsense about a knife?

The boys ended up having to pay a fine.

Three years later, Mary Deasy and Hannah O'Connor presented a united front when they were charged with stealing wood on the Dunscombe estate. When called to testify, the man to whom Dunscombe had sold the wood said he'd given the defendants permission to take limbs—contradicting an earlier statement to the police. Mary Deasy got a laugh in court when she labeled the police sergeant testifying against them a "great rogue" for swearing a false oath. Case dismissed.[10]

Cork's smash-mouth politics added to the family's troubles. Patrick O'Connor was cycling home one evening in August 1911 when one Denis Crowley rushed up and slugged him in the jaw. Down went O'Connor, down went the bike, and down came a flurry of kicks and blows from Crowley and several kinsmen. Somebody even bit Patrick's fingers.

Patrick's brother John, also heading home on a bike, stumbled across the donnybrook and tried to help, but he, too, quickly went down, punched in the eye, kicked in the ribs, and smashed in the mouth—he emerged minus a tooth. The O'Connors brought charges against Denis Crowley, John Crowley, and Hannah Crowley.

The Crowley clan filed countercharges, saying the O'Connors had started it all, and that John had waved a penknife. John denied it all—the penknife he didn't menace O'Driscoll with in 1903 was apparently the same penknife he didn't wave at the Crowleys in 1911.

A police sergeant testified that the O'Connors were "respectable people," and that the Crowley's were anything but. The O'Connors' lawyer said the whole thing "originally arose as an election row."[11] The Crowleys may have gotten the best of the brawl, but they were pummeled by the judge—all three were convicted and sentenced to two months' hard labor.

There was nearly as much partisan bad blood as there was Beamish stout in the Cork of 1911—the city faced a political vendetta every bit as fierce as the O'Connor-Deasy feud. Since 1908, the once-dominant Irish Parliamentary Party of John Redmond had been struggling to keep control of the city in the face of a strong challenge from the All-For-Ireland League of William O'Brien, a longtime fixture of politics in the area. A 1910 general election saw the two sides clashing almost nightly. As one historian put it, street fighting was "a strand of Cork's political DNA."[12]

It's not clear which party the O'Connors favored, but if one had to bet, the odds would be on the Redmond political machine—the elder O'Connor held a municipal job in a city where patronage ruled employment.[13] And there is evidence that the Deasys backed Redmond's rival. In August 1904, William Deasy seconded O'Brien's nomination to Parliament in papers filed in Cork.[14] Political differences may have helped fuel the feud between the two families.

And politics wasn't the only source of tension in the late summer of 1911 when Patrick O'Connor took that punch to the jaw. Another conflict that likely involved him—a railroad strike—broke out the same month as his scuffle.

In August 1911, O'Connor was an eighteen-year-old railway fireman, shoveling coal into the furnace of a locomotive. On August 18, a rail labor dispute in Dublin resulted in a strike that quickly spread and was just as quickly resolved. But the strike inspired lumberyard workers to demand higher pay and better conditions, so employers locked them out and brought in replacements.[15] In September, some railway workers refused to handle goods from a lumberyard involved in the lockout. The workers were fired by the Great Southern and Western Railway Company, which triggered a sweeping walkout all along the line—in Dublin, Cork, Limerick, and Waterford.

Management took a hard stand, bringing in British troops and Protestant replacement workers from Ulster. One traveler on the Dublin-Cork line described the army of occupation: "It looked as if Ireland was turned into a military camp. . . . All the signal boxes, pumping stations, and railway bridges were guarded by troops with loaded firearms."

Backed by the army's bayonets, the Great Southern was intent on not just winning the strike, but on making it a teachable moment for the strikers. It insisted that the replacement workers would stay when the strike ended—which meant that 10 percent of the old workforce would lose their jobs. The battered union swallowed its pride, cut its losses, and returned to work in early October. Lesson learned.

As an eighteen-year-old, Patrick O'Connor may well have been among the 10 percent who lost their jobs. We know that he eventually moved on to a job in a department store in the center of Cork.

Here then, is a portrait of the O'Connors of Mount Desert, in many ways a typical working-class Irish family as the second decade of the twentieth century dawned. In 1911, John, the patriarch, is forty-eight and working as an engine driver for Cork city.[16] Hannah, at fifty-two, is keeping house and sometimes working at the nearby mental asylum. Three of her four sons—John Jr., twenty-five; Patrick, eighteen; and Michael, sixteen—are still at home, all of them working, Michael as a porter in a store.

One son is gone, and another soon will be: Seventeen-year-old Jeremiah died in 1908, and they lost John in December 1911 at age twenty-five.[17] Such deaths were not uncommon in a city where tuberculosis could kill close to three hundred in a year.[18]

The surviving O'Connor boys did the kind of things Irish boys do. Paddy played Gaelic football for the local team, Clogheen.[19] His brother Michael was forever getting into trouble with the law over his obsession with the ancient Irish sport of road bowling. The game has been compared to golf with cannonballs, except there are no clubs, and no greens—as the name suggests, it's played on roads, with the goal of covering a set course with the fewest shots.[20]

Despite the constabulary's disapproval, County Cork has long been a bastion of road bowling, and Michael did his level best to keep it that way. He was given a police summons for bowling in August 1914 and landed back in court twice in the spring of 1916 for the same offense—in March and May. He was at it again in 1919, when he was fined ten shillings in August. He didn't even let his family's long-standing feud with the Deasys get in the way—in the case from May 1916, Willie Deasy was summoned for aiding and abetting him, and fined two shillings.[21]

By sheer coincidence, these court appearances roughly coincide with a series of events that would turn the O'Connor family, Cork, all of Ireland, and much of the world upside down. Michael's game of bowls at Coolymurraghue on August 2, 1914, came just as World War I was erupting; Great Britain entered the war two days later. His court appearances in the spring of 1916 straddled the Easter Uprising in Dublin, when Irish rebels launched a doomed fight for independence in April of that year. And August 1919, when Michael was fined ten shillings for bowling, just happened to be the month when some reckon the Irish Republican Army was officially born.

A City Transformed

In just six years, the Cork that the O'Connors knew would become unrecognizable. In 1914, when World War I broke out, the city was known as "Khaki Cork" for its ties to the British military establishment.[22] The British Army's massive Victoria Barracks crowned a hill on the city's North Side; outside the city lay one of the Royal Navy's biggest bases, at Queenstown (now Cobh).

By the end of the decade the city and county were "rebel Cork," one of the main battlegrounds of the Irish revolution.

That much change cannot happen that quickly without creating a swirl of conflicting loyalties. As one historian put it, "driven by events, parties chose their ally of the moment, revealing an unexpected fluidity of loyalty and identity in Cork."[23] What was true of organizations and political parties was true of families and individuals. It was certainly true of Cruxy.

In the years leading up to World War I, politics in Cork centered on the competition between Redmond's Irish Parliamentary Party and O'Brien's All-For-Ireland League. The rivalry boiled down to different visions of Ireland's future as embodied by Home Rule, which would have created an Irish legislature to deal with the island's domestic policies, while retaining Irish representation in the British Parliament.

In 1911, Ireland was about 74 percent Catholic and 26 percent Protestant. Catholics tended to support Home Rule. But much of the north of Ireland— Ulster—was dominated by Protestants, the descendants of English and Scottish settlers brought in to pacify the rebel province. They vehemently opposed Home Rule, fearing they would face discrimination in a Dublin Parliament dominated by southern Catholic nationalists.

John Redmond's Irish Party was not inclined to make concessions to these Ulster "Unionists." O'Brien's All-for-Ireland League, on the other hand, emphasized an Ulster policy of "conference, conciliation and consent."[24] This was the heart of the dispute that landed Paddy O'Connor a punch in the summer of 1911.

In 1912 the Irish Party held the balance of power in Parliament, so after multiple failed attempts going back decades, a Home Rule bill won initial approval—and Unionists moved to the brink of armed rebellion. Half a million people signed the Ulster Covenant, refusing to recognize Parliament's authority in the matter; a hundred thousand joined the Ulster Volunteers, a Unionist militia determined to resist Home Rule.

In the south, O'Brien's All-for-Ireland movement opposed the Home Rule bill, appalled at the prospect of civil war. Its credibility among southern nationalists was ruined. Redmond's Irish Party went in the other direction, forming its own militia, the Irish Volunteers, to defend Home Rule from the Ulster Volunteers. By 1914, with Home Rule due to take effect, both groups were running in guns from Germany, preparing to slug it out in a civil war, if need be. Elements of the British Army's officer corps all but mutinied over plans to move against the rebellious Ulster Volunteers.

At the last moment, disaster was forestalled by catastrophe. In late July 1914, the biggest war Europe had ever known erupted.

Chapter 3

War and Rebellion

THE GREAT WAR came on like a pandemic—localized at first, but soon raging out of control, fatally infectious in a way that defied the meager limits of human imagination. Leaders thought they could control it. Far-off non-combatants thought it wouldn't affect them. The young thought they were invulnerable. Almost everyone thought it would be over soon.

All were deluded, and Ireland was far from immune to the fever dreams.

From Belfast to Cork, the war quickly rid Ireland of large numbers of men who believed the island's rightful place was in the British Empire. In the north, the Ulster Volunteers, whose loyalty to the United Kingdom had nearly ended in rebellion, enlisted en masse. In Cork, O'Brien's All-for-Ireland League, always sympathetic to northern Unionists, sponsored a recruitment rally that drew a thousand.[1]

O'Brien's rival, Redmond, joined the bandwagon, in a move that divided the Irish Volunteers. While the bulk of the organization consisted of Redmond's followers, the Volunteers had been infiltrated from the start by a small, dedicated band of separatists. They wanted no part of defending an empire they were plotting to violently quit.

The organization behind all this plotting was the Irish Republican Brotherhood, or IRB, a secret, oath-bound society of separatist revolutionaries that dated back to 1858. It had an American counterpart, the Fenian Brotherhood, founded in New York that same year. By late 1858 there was a panicked British hunt in Cork and Kerry for members of a trans-Atlantic secret society dedicated to wresting Ireland from the United Kingdom, the

New York Tribune reported. (The article was written by a German fellow named Karl Marx.)[2]

Rebel secret societies sprouted in Ireland the way mushrooms flourish in a forest, Marx observed. But in the past, they tended to be regional, rural, and focused on issues like land tenure and sectarian strife. What had London worried, Marx wrote, was "something quite new, quite unknown, and the more awful for all that"—an international revolutionary organization.

As one historian put it: "From now on, British and Irish alike had to contend with a third party, the United States, the world's ascendant nation, with its millions of exiled Irish, ready, willing and increasingly able to use their votes, and their spare pennies, on behalf of the people they left behind, and the cause they didn't."[3]

Thus was born the terrible beauty of the Irish Republican Brotherhood.

But at first the most terrible thing about these international revolutionaries was their track record.

The American Fenians, many of them Union Army veterans of the Civil War, invaded Canada in 1866, and failed. The IRB staged an uprising in Ireland the next year and failed. The Fenians had another go at Canada in 1870, and failed.

But instead of disbanding after all these debacles, the organization soldiered on for decades, blowing on the dying embers of rebellion.

In 1908, the hidebound Cork branch, or "circle," had to be reborn. The organization wanted young plotters, not old prattlers, so it simply bypassed the IRB circle in Cork and set up a new one.[4] You can do that sort of thing when a society is secret, and the geezers were never the wiser.

By the time World War I came along, the Cork IRB had attracted a new generation—among them Sean O'Hegarty, whose brother was on the secret society's supreme council; Tomas MacCurtain, who was active in the Irish Volunteers; and Martin Donovan, the first of the Cork Volunteers. Donovan, a laborer in his twenties who lived with his aunt and uncle on Peacock Lane, was a man of few words, fearless but never foolhardy, ever cool in a tight spot.[5]

The war these men wanted was not with Germany.

The issue came to a head at a meeting of one thousand Irish Volunteers in Cork on August 30, 1914. The two sides debated, and about 930 opted to defend the empire.[6] As the rebel playwright Brendan Behan quipped, the first item on the agenda of any new Irish organization was "the Split," and that was certainly the case here. A small, distilled band of seventy separatists splintered off to form their own group, keeping the name Irish Volunteers (Redmond's group became the National Volunteers). Similar scenes happened across Ireland as the Volunteer movement divided. By December, over forty thousand of Redmond's Volunteers had enlisted, confident that their sacrifice for Britain would be rewarded with Home Rule for Ireland.

With the war just a month old, the separatists opted for another path: rebellion. England's difficulty was seen as Ireland's opportunity, and the rebels planned to seize it before the war ended.[7]

The course of subsequent events seemed to flow in a revolutionary direction. While the separatist Irish Volunteers were sometimes spat upon in Cork immediately after the split, the situation changed as the war dragged on. Sapped by enlistments in the British Army and lacking any official role in the defense of Ireland, Redmond's National Volunteers withered alongside hopes for a quick Allied victory. By the fall of 1915, both had all but evaporated.

In Cork and elsewhere, the rival Irish Volunteers were resurgent, buoyed by antiwar sentiment, and an energetic recruiter, Terence MacSwiney. A longtime republican who joined the IRB in 1915, he went to work as a full-time Irish Volunteer recruiter in Cork in July of that year. As a result, one Volunteer recalled, new units "cropped up like mushrooms"—a phrase with a familiar ring in this context.[8]

Among the new recruits in 1915 were Patrick A. Murray, known as Pa for his initials, and Danny Healy. Murray, from Rockwell Lane, just off Sunday's Well Road, was a six-foot, one-inch scholarship student at University College Cork and the nephew of Fred Murray, a Volunteer organizer. Pa was known for his laughing good humor—pleasant, silent when he needed to be, and efficient.[9] Healy was the son of a hackney driver who in 1911 was living with his parents and three siblings at 156 Blarney Street. A teetotaler, he worked as a bootmaker and played Gaelic football.

The Volunteers drew heavily from members of the Gaelic Athletic Association. One man said of his unit: "Every Volunteer in A Company was either a hurler or a Gaelic footballer."[10]

The Volunteer oath was the first step in the evolution from sportsman to gunmen. A familiar series of milestones marked the progress of Irish secret societies heading down the road to violence. After a secret oath came drilling and training, then raids for arms, because what good was all the drilling and training if you didn't have guns? The raids for arms inevitably led some of those raided to complain to the authorities, and that led to retaliatory attacks on the "informers," and clashes with the police.

That last point is worth keeping in mind, because while the War for Independence is frequently cast as an Anglo-Irish conflict, it was in many respects a civil war, one that pitted Irish rebels against Irish constables.

The Easter Rising

The first phase of the struggle for independence, the Easter Rising of 1916, was very much an Irish vs. British affair. The IRB had settled on an insurrection very shortly after Britain entered World War I. Less than a year and half later, it launched a doomed rebellion that the British military crushed in less than a week, leaving hundreds dead and the center of Dublin a smoking ruin.

In a sense, the rising ended up as less a rational military operation than an emotional performance in blood. In a land where the line between rebellion and folk drama had been blurred for generations, it offered a familiar plot line: the resurrection of the Irish nation via a blood sacrifice around a holiday.

Agrarian rebels, going back to the Whiteboys and Molly Maguires, had often donned the costumes of mummers when they launched attacks timed to major holidays.[11] The mummers' play always featured a battle, a killing, and the slain man rising to fight again—and in many cases, the resurrected was none other than that symbol of Ireland, Saint Patrick. Patrick Pearse, the leader of the Easter Uprising, echoed the theme less than a year before Easter 1916: "Life springs from death, and from the graves of patriot men and women spring living nations."

When, in the rising's opening act, Pearse read the Proclamation of the Irish Republic, the dead were mentioned in the very first sentence: "In the name of God and of the dead generations from which she receives her old tradition of nationhood, Ireland, through us, summons her children to her flag and strikes for her freedom."

Pearse excelled at drama. His ability to organize an effective rebellion was another matter entirely. The problem was that while the IRB had thoroughly infiltrated the leadership of the Irish Volunteers, the head of the organization, Eoin MacNeill, was neither a member nor an enthusiastic supporter of the insurrection.

When he caught wind of the real purpose of the "maneuvers" that Pearse, as director of operations, had ordered for Easter Sunday, MacNeill waffled a bit, then issued a countermanding order. The deciding factor was the Royal Navy's interception of a ship that was to deliver thousands of German weapons to the rebels in County Kerry.[12]

MacNeill's move effectively limited the major action to Dublin, and even there forced a one-day delay.

On Easter Monday, the Irish Volunteers seized the General Post Office in the center of Dublin, aided by a leftist workers militia, James Connolly's

Irish Citizens Army. Elsewhere in the city, the rebels grabbed the Four Courts, Dublin's judicial center; St. Stephen's Green; and Boland's Mill, among other sites.[13]

Outside the post office, Pearse proclaimed the Irish Republic to some curious onlookers, and then Volunteers started smashing windows—nothing says "revolution" like the sound of breaking glass.

Among the rebels turning Pearse's words into reality: a big fellow from Cork named Michael Collins, who served as an aide to Joseph Plunkett, the rising's main military planner,[14] and a lone American—John Kilgallon of Rockaway, New York. The twenty-three-year-old son of immigrants from County Mayo, Kilgallon served as a messenger for Pearse, his old school-master from an Irish-language academy in Dublin, St. Enda's. When they marched into the General Post Office, Kilgallon loudly announced, in his New York accent, "Holy gee! This ain't no half-arsed revolution! This is the business."[15]

The odd part was that Kilgallon had come to Ireland to get *out* of a fracas, not into one. His father owned a garage, and in 1912 Kilgallon "borrowed" a client's roadster for a late-night joy ride with some friends. It all ended in a crash, four serious injuries, and a pile of legal trouble.

That's why the Kilgallon family was so open to sending young Johnny off to St. Enda's when Pearse recruited him during a 1914 trip to the United States.

Pearse was far from alone in having visited the US—it seemed there was scarcely a leader of the uprising who hadn't seen the Statue of Liberty. Tom Clarke, the old Fenian whose name appeared first on the Proclamation of the Republic, lived in New York from 1899 to 1907, and became a US citizen. Connolly, the leader of the Irish Citizens Army, spent eight years in America from 1902 to 1910, much of it in New York and environs. Eamon de Valera, the commander at Boland's Mill, was born in New York. Plunkett included the United States in his extensive world travels.[16]

On the second day of the rising, Tuesday, the British started punching back with artillery, and the pounding got worse as the days went by—the big buildings seized by the rebels made for big targets. The British Army was in no mood to tread lightly in Ireland while the Germans were pressing hard with poison gas attacks in France.[17] When a new British commander, General John Maxwell, arrived in Dublin on Friday, he declared, "If necessary, I shall not hesitate to destroy all buildings within any area occupied by the rebels."[18]

By the end of the day the General Post Office was ablaze. Collins, the big fellow from Cork, had his pants burned by a falling timber; Kilgallon, the New Yorker, was running around like mad, trying to put out fires on the roof.[19] The rebels had to flee the burning ruin under heavy fire. The roof Kilgallon had tried to save collapsed, and on Saturday, so did the rebellion (though some Volunteers held out until Sunday).

When it was all over, hundreds were dead—rebels, British soldiers, and civilians. By the time the British stopped executing the leaders, like Pearse, Connolly, Clarke, and Plunkett, the toll came close to five hundred. The survivors, like Collins, Kilgallon, and de Valera—the executions were halted just before de Valera faced a firing squad—were shipped off to Frongoch, an internment camp in Wales, or various prisons.

Dublin had made its stand. But while Dublin rose and fought, Cork stumbled and fell.

Pa Murray, sworn in to the IRB the week before the rising, turned out on Easter with Martin Donovan, Danny Healy, and the other Cork Volunteers. "The Cork City Battalion paraded at Sheaves Street and marched to Capitol railway station in the city and thence by train to Crookstown in West Cork," Healy recalled. They were planning to link up with Volunteers from neighboring Kerry so they could arm themselves with guns being run in by the German ship.

In the tiny crossroads village of Beal na Blath, everything went to hell.

"At Beal na Blath a motor car arrived," one Volunteer recalled. "Terry MacSwiney, we understood, came in the car with the countermand from Eoin MacNeill."[20] The men proceeded on to Macroom, joking about the fine homes and estates that they'd seize, then disbanded and took a train home.

It was back to Cork, and to shame and humiliation.

With Dublin up in arms, the British military demanded that the Cork Volunteers surrender theirs. To prevent bloodshed, the Roman Catholic bishop of Cork brokered a deal—the Volunteers would surrender their guns to the mayor, at least until the rising was over. They did and felt terrible about it. Pa Murray said he managed to switch a few dummy rifles for the real things before the handover, but it was scant consolation.[21] "The hour had come and we, in Cork, had done nothing," another republican bitterly recalled.[22]

The shame of 1916 would have huge consequences for Cork republicans. Now they had something to prove.

Raids and Reorganization

The failed Easter Rising no more deterred the IRB than the failed Fenian rising in 1867 did. The familiar rituals of oath-taking, drilling, and raiding for arms resumed with a new intensity. Early in 1917, Danny Healy was sworn in to the brotherhood's Cork circle.

In September, he was on lookout duty in a raid for arms at the Cork Grammar School.[23] An elite secondary school run by the Church of Ireland, the school housed an officers' training corps, along with dozens of rifles.

"About twenty of our lads took part in the raid which resulted in the capture of about thirty rifles," Healy said. The guns were carried off by IRB stalwarts Denis MacNeilus, Martin Donovan, and Daniel "Sandow" Donovan, among others. Healy later helped move some of the guns to Clogheen, a rural area just west of the city that included Mount Desert where the O'Connors lived. In addition to lifting the guns, the men had lifted the organization's morale.

"It once and for all wiped out whatever stigma was there on the arms surrender of 1916," one republican said.[24]

Early in 1918, Britain began to consider conscription in Ireland to fill the ranks of an army depleted by four years of grinding trench warfare. A military draft was a stress test of any government's legitimacy, and the Irish rarely handed out passing grades. Not in 1793, when Catholics rioted because they believed that Protestant sheriffs were drafting them first. Not in New York during the American Civil War, when Irish immigrants played a leading role in bloody antidraft riots. And certainly not in the hard-coal fields of Pennsylvania, where the Molly Maguires were resurrected around the same time, after a Protestant Republican draft official set unfairly high quotas for townships filled with Irish Catholic Democrats and mine labor activists.[25]

In 1918, the reaction was similar.

The threat of a draft led to "a big influx into the Volunteers," Pa Murray recalled. "Companies were split up and new companies were formed. The city was divided into two battalions—1st Battalion, north of the River Lee, and 2nd Battalion, south of same."[26]

Murray, Martin Donovan, and Danny Healy were assigned to the 1st Battalion's new C Company, which was based on the western fringe of Cork city, where the working-class rowhouses of Blarney Street bleed into the farm fields of Clogheen north of the River Lee. The neighborhood was filled with the sort of young militants that one leading rebel had in mind when he spoke of the city's IRA men as "truculent, sturdy characters without a trace of subservience."[27]

In November, the tensions between these truculent Volunteers and the constabulary boiled over, thanks to Denis MacNeilus, a hard case from Donegal. As armorer for the Cork city Volunteers, he'd pledged that if the coppers ever raided his house, he'd fight to defend the arms in his care.

They came for him on November 4, 1918, and sure enough, in the crazed melee that followed, MacNeilus plugged the head constable, Clarke, in the stomach. It looked like Clarke would die from his wound—and that Mac-Neilus would swing on the gallows.

But not if Martin Donovan could help it.

The Escape Artist

Donovan went to war on the very day that the rest of the world stopped fighting. It was the most thrilling moment of his life.

Just hours after the official end of World War I on November 11, 1918, Donovan and several other men broke MacNeilus out of His Britannic Majesty's Male Prison in Cork.

The brains of the operation was Florrie O'Donoghue. He and MacNeilus had been thick as thieves since the year before, when MacNeilus was placed in charge of a Volunteer Cyclist Company and nominated O'Donoghue as his first lieutenant.[28] MacNeilus may have been good with guns, but Florrie's brain was one of the sharpest weapons in the Volunteers' arsenal, and after a couple of visits to the Cork jail to get the lay of the place, he came up with an escape plan.

It wouldn't be easy, for it required split-second timing and a lot of men—at least six inside, and more outside. Getting into the prison to visit someone was a three-step process, so busting MacNeilus out of there was going to require three stages as well.

Here's how it worked: To visit a prisoner, you knocked at the imposing front gate of the prison grounds. You were admitted and escorted across the yard to a small structure that served as a waiting room in between the front gate and an interior gate. Meanwhile the prisoner was taken from his cell to a visiting room. Once the prisoner was in the visiting room, one of the guards would unlock the interior gate, usher the visitors through it, relock the gate and escort them to the visiting room in the prison building.

To break someone out of the place, O'Donoghue realized, you needed to briefly control the visiting room, the waiting room. and the two gates. His plan: Send in three two-man teams a few minutes apart.[29] One team would be in the visiting room; the other two in the waiting room. At the designated moment, the two-man team in the visiting room would subdue the guard there, take his keys, leave the locked visiting room and the prison proper with MacNeilus, and head to the interior gate. There they would be met by the two other teams, who, after subduing the guard in the waiting room and grabbing his keys, would unlock the interior gate, and rush the three men who'd been in the visiting room to the front gate. All seven would exit the front gate after locking everything behind them, keeping the keys and making their getaway on bicycles. A big covering party of Volunteers would be waiting outside to cut the phone lines and provide assistance, if needed.

Everybody involved needed steel nerves, but especially the two men who were going furthest into the prison and performing the actual rescue. Joe Murphy was chosen for the task, and insisted on the cool, poker-faced Martin Donovan as the second. They were all armed. It all went according to plan. Nearly.

At 3:25 p.m., Donovan and Murphy knocked at the front gate of the prison and were escorted to the waiting room. Five minutes later, a second pair of Volunteers were escorted into the waiting room, and three minutes later, the third pair. So far, so good.

Then came the unexpected.

An army lorry drove up to the prison entrance and the driver found himself in the midst of several watchful, hard-eyed men milling about with hands in their coat pockets—the rebel squad Florrie O'Donoghue had stationed outside in case something went wrong. The young army driver, realizing something was very wrong, tried to drive away. He was promptly yanked out of the cab and handed over to Raymond Kennedy, who kept his revolver—and his hand—in his pocket.

"I wish you would take your hands out of your pockets," the nervous young soldier said,

"I prefer to keep them in there," the equally nervous Kennedy replied.[30]

That truck was likely the source of some tense moments for Donovan and Murphy inside. As they were about to be escorted from the waiting building to the prison, a party of armed British soldiers came through the main entrance—probably from the lorry. In the waiting room, six hands went into six pockets, fingers tightening around pistol grips as the men waited to see if the soldiers were headed for the waiting area.

They weren't. Six trigger fingers relaxed.[31]

Donovan later told a buddy that no words could describe his feelings at the heart-stopping instant when he saw the soldiers. He had another moment like that when he and Murphy made it into the visiting room, and the guard locked them in.[32]

The visiting room was cut in two—prisoners on one side of a low barrier, visitors on the other. Donovan and Murphy made perfunctory conversation with the prisoner for a few minutes, then announced that they had to leave, to catch a train. A confused MacNeilus wanted to keep talking, but the visitors insisted they needed to go.

As the guard produced a key to unlock the visiting room, Donovan and Murphy sandbagged him. He slumped to the floor, out cold. They unlocked the door and somebody yelled, "Jump, Mac." The prisoner vaulted over the divide, and out the door the three went. Murphy had to go back when he realized he had left it unlocked.

And that wasn't the only problem with a key.

The boys in the waiting room took down the guard and tied him up, as planned. They grabbed his keys, as planned. They disconnected the phone, as planned. They headed for the interior gate, as planned. What wasn't planned was that the key wouldn't turn in the lock of the gate. They took turns, seconds ticking away in an operation that demanded split-second timing.

Then, just as Donovan, Murphy and MacNeilus came hurrying toward them, the key turned, and the gate opened. They locked the interior gate behind them and headed for the front entrance, locking that, too, as they exited.

Then they were all in the street, reunited with the covering party outside, everybody rejoicing, when suddenly they looked around and came to a horrifying realization.

The freed prisoner was nowhere to be seen.

MacNeilus had simply jumped on a bike and pedaled off, assuming that the main idea of a prison break was to get the hell away from the prison. When he realized that he was alone, he turned around and headed back, but by then the rescue party had dispersed on their own bikes. While his friend Florrie mounted a desperate search of the city for him, MacNeilus holed up in the home of a republican sympathizer in Clogheen. Finally he got word to O'Donoghue, and came in from the cold.[33]

The *Cork Examiner* called the breakout "one of the most extraordinary and carefully planned coups of its kind ever brought off."

In the streets that night, British soldiers riotously celebrated the end of the war. "It was a rowdy night in Cork," one Volunteer recalled. "Intoxicated Tommies from Victoria Barracks whooped it up in style with beshawled dames, whose husbands, brothers and sons were 'doing their bit' overseas."[34]

But even as the British toasted their victory in the bloodiest war Europe had ever seen, Cork republicans were quietly raising a glass to their bloodless triumph at the prison.

The caper separated the men from the boys in the republican movement in Cork—and it was the boys who took over. Longtime leaders like Pa Murray's uncle, Fred, had objected to the plan, put off by the weapons and the risk.[35] In the aftermath, they faded away and the vacuum was filled by a younger, less gun-shy generation.

The same thing happened on a much bigger scale the month after the jailbreak. When the war ended, the government in London called a national parliamentary election for December 1918. "The results were astonishing," Pa Murray said—a landslide in Ireland for the young upstarts in the separatist party, Sinn Fein, buried the old guard of Redmond's Irish Parliamentary Party, forever altering the landscape of Irish history.[36]

Instead of heading to London, the victorious Sinn Fein parliamentary candidates convened in Dublin to form an Irish Parliament—Dail Eireann—on January 23, 1919. That same day, Volunteers in Tipperary killed two policemen in Soloheadbeg. The war for independence was on, and Tomas MacCurtain, the commander of Cork's Irish Volunteers, was elected lord mayor.

By August, members of the Irish Volunteers were taking an oath of allegiance to the Dail, and thus the Volunteers became the Irish Republican Army.[37]

Through it all, Martin Donovan turned jailbreaks into something of a specialty. He was there in the spring of 1919, when Sean Moylan, a rebel leader and future government minister, was smuggled out of the Cork District Lunatic Asylum on C Company's turf. Moylan had been jailed but was transferred to the asylum after an impressive ensemble performance by other imprisoned rebels, who told the guards, "He's a lunatic and every relation of his died in a lunatic asylum." Moylan got into the act by hurling food and screaming "Poison, poison."[38]

The jailers bought the story and sent Moylan to the far less secure asylum. "A few days later the hospital had a number of visitors," Moylan said. "They took up positions quietly at doorways and in the hospital corridors. Ten minutes later I was speeding to the mountains in the company of my comrades. My sanity had returned."

Donovan was also there in late April, when Dick Murphy was rescued from a hospital after being wounded in an accidental explosion in a rebel bomb factory. And he was there on January 13, 1920, when Edward Horgan, a republican prisoner who'd been transferred to a hospital for a tonsillectomy, made his getaway, disguised as a nurse.[39]

Aside from Donovan, Murray, and Healy, C Company had a hard core of active members, among them, Willie Deasy, Paddy O'Connor's neighbor in Mount Desert, and Jerry Mullane, of 227 Blarney Street. Both would die as a result of O'Connor's betrayal. Mullane had been a Volunteer since 1914, had done two stints in jail, and had gone on hunger strike.[40] By 1919 and 1920, he and Willie Deasy were among C Company's most active raiders from arms.[41]

The IRA vs. the RIC

The uptick in arms raids came just as the Royal Irish Constabulary was feeling the strain of the struggle. Shunned as traitors to Ireland, many constables fled the barracks and shed their uniforms, either resigning or retiring. Their departure cost the crown forces not just manpower, but vital local intelligence.

To deal with the manpower shortage, London in early 1920 began a vast recruitment effort, signing up thousands of former soldiers from throughout Britain and Ireland to fill the barracks. They were quickly tagged "the Black and Tans" for their motley uniforms, and just as quickly developed a reputation as a brutal and ill-disciplined army of occupation. Over the summer, the RIC was further reinforced by the creation of the Auxiliary Division, a paramilitary strike force composed of over two thousand former British military officers.[42]

Those moves addressed the manpower crisis, but the British replacements faced a much bigger problem—a dearth of local knowledge and reliable intelligence. For that, they had to turn to informers. Which meant that for the IRA, spying on the police and hunting for informers was now a top priority—and its Cork units developed a reputation for ruthless action against spies real and imagined.

"Early in 1920, practically the whole of C Company was engaged watching the comings and goings of the RIC and Black and Tans at the various barracks in our district," Healy said. "Particular attention was paid to civilians seen to be entering or leaving barracks. Reports on these activities were then forwarded to the Battalion Intelligence officer."[43]

In early February 1920, C Company got word that the police from Blarney, acting on a tip, were descending on their weapons stash, or dump, in Clogheen. That wouldn't do at all. Pa Murray, by now the company captain, rushed out to intercept the constabulary, along with Danny Healy, Willie Deasy, Tom Dennehy, and several others.

"We were all armed with revolvers," Healy said. "When we arrived on the scene the raid was over, and the police were making their way towards Blarney. We tried to intercept them, but they had got too much of a start.

However, we saw them and opened fire with revolvers, but we were too far distant to be effective."[44]

They failed to stop the raid, but the boys of C Company did something crucial that day, something they'd never done before: They'd gone into battle, as a unit.

Chapter 4

▚

The Battle for Cork

WHEN IT CAME to doing the very worst, Pa Murray, Martin Donovan, and Danny Healy were among the very best. As one comrade put it: "Any shooting that was to be done, Healy was on it."[1] Pa Murray said of Donovan's frequent role as gunman: "Martin Donovan was in everything; that's about the size of it."[2]

To break Britain's hold on Ireland, the rebels needed, first and foremost, to break Britain's front line of defense, the police. Murray, Healy, and Donovan, it could be fairly said, were the terror of the Royal Irish Constabulary.

Those potshots at the police in the Clogheen countryside were just the start. At various times, members of the trio strolled into a club and gunned down the police commissioner for the province of Munster. They gunned down two other policemen as they were boarding a tram after work. They kidnapped a constable attending Mass, then let him go when it turned out they had grabbed the wrong man. They took part in any number of raids on police barracks and executed more than one spy.

The spiral of violence began with the killings of several policemen and spun out of control with the assassination of the lord mayor of Cork by several cops.

On March 16, two constables were fatally shot as they returned from Lenten devotions at the Catholic church in Toomevara, County Tipperary.[3] Among those attending the funerals was Detective Joseph Murtagh of Cork, who had a reputation for being none too gentle with republican prisoners.

His tender mercies were currently being visited upon Martin Condon, an IRA man who'd been captured the previous month after an attack on a police barracks.[4]

As Pa Murray put it: "Condon was being held prisoner in the military barracks in Cork at the time, and it was known that this detective was using extreme methods on him in order to procure information."[5] The "extreme methods" included dosing suspects with chloroform as a sort of truth serum for interrogations.[6]

This was not to be tolerated, so two men from Murray's C Company—J. J. O'Connell and Christy MacSwiney—were dispatched to eliminate Murtagh, who was gunned down March 19 on Pope's Quay in the center of Cork after he returned from the funeral.[7]

This, too, was not to be tolerated, and the reaction from crown forces was swift. Just hours after the Murtagh shooting, several armed men disguised with blackened faces came hammering at the front door of the lord mayor of Cork, Tomas MacCurtain, who also happened to be the commander of the Cork brigade of the Irish Republican Army. Armed men with blackened faces battering at the door in the wee hours is one of the recurring nightmares of Irish history, and it rarely turns out well for those inside.

This was no exception.

MacCurtain's wife let the intruders in, on the unmistaken assumption that they were the police. Two rushed past her upstairs to the hall outside the lord mayor's bedroom, shouting "Come out, Curtain." He did, and for his cooperation was rewarded with three bullets to the chest.[8]

Thus died the leading republican activist in Cork.

A coroner's jury, leavened with IRA men, offered a stunning finding in the case: "The murder was organized and carried out by the Royal Irish Constabulary, officially directed by the British Government, and we return a verdict of willful murder against David Lloyd George, Prime Minister of England; Lord French, Lord Lieutenant of Ireland; Ian McPherson, late Chief Secretary of Ireland; Acting Inspector General Smith of the Royal Irish Constabulary; Divisional Inspector Clayton of the Royal Irish Constabulary; District Inspector Swanzy and some unknown members of the Royal Irish Constabulary."[9]

No one rushed to slap handcuffs on the prime minister or the lord lieutenant, but the IRA was quietly working on its own form of rough justice.

By April, some of the "unknown members of the Royal Irish Constabulary" had become known. Pa Murray recalled: "The Brigade intelligence Officer, Florrie O'Donoghue, became aware about this time of the identity of two members of the murder gang who assassinated Tomas MacCurtain.

These police were stationed in the Lower Road barracks, and it was decided to attack them."[10]

In the crosshairs: Sergeant Denis Garvey and Constable Daniel Harrington.

If you are going to embark on the awful business of killing human beings, there is probably no better target than political assassins to quell the moral qualms. The job, like a lot of the dirty work in Cork, fell to the men of C Company—they weren't from the neighborhood, so they were less likely to be recognized.

Murray had the boys stake out the Lower Road Barracks, and they determined that Garvey and Harrington, along with a third policeman, Constable Doyle, regularly used a tram car that ran in front of the barracks.

The attack was set for the night of May 12. On hand were the company's stalwarts, including Pa Murray, Martin Donovan, Dan Healy, Willie Deasy, and Mick Bowles. A Volunteer who was related to Bowles, Jerry Mahoney, acted as guide. Two men—one dressed as a woman—were placed across the road, opposite the barracks door, "pretending to be lovers," as Healy put it.[11] (Pa Murray's sister, Eily, provided the skirt and stockings for the disguise.)[12] And just to be sure, a gunman was placed on either side of the barracks door.

Pa Murray described what happened next: "Myself and Martin Donovan were at the tram stop and, when we saw the RIC party leave the barracks and move towards the stop, we entered the tram. They entered the train at the stop and, as they stepped onto the platform, we shot the two wanted men (Sergeant Garvey and Constable Harrington)."[13]

Doyle, the third policeman, was wounded. He wasn't on the hit list.

The next night, seventeen members of C Company were on guard duty outside the home of Terence MacSwiney, who replaced MacCurtain both as the lord mayor of Cork and as commander of the city's IRA brigade—they wanted to ensure the coppers didn't pull a repeat of the MacCurtain vigilante killing. But MacSwiney wasn't destined to die so easy a death. In his inaugural speech as lord mayor, he famously declared, "It is not those who can inflict the most, but those who can suffer the most, who will conquer."

He may have been thinking of MacCurtain, but his words proved prophetic.

The Blarney Barracks Attack

Just weeks after the tram-car killings, on June 1, the IRA stepped up its war on the constabulary by hitting the police where they lived—in their barracks.

For Pa Murray and Martin Donovan, it was once more into the breach, and this time Murray got himself blown into the next room for his troubles.

The target was the Blarney Barracks of the Royal Irish Constabulary, about six miles from Cork. Murray was at the forefront, along with Daniel "Sandow" Donovan—the nickname came from his resemblance to a famed German bodybuilder, Eugen Sandow. They and a few others entered a hotel adjoining the barracks and planted explosives against the connecting wall.

"The plan was that the wall would be breached by a charge of guncotton and that three of us, including myself, would go through the breach first, to be followed by the other men," Murray said. "Breaching the wall would have brought us directly into the dayroom of the barracks."

The attacks didn't go as planned—the boys were not exactly experts in the bomb department.

"When the guncotton exploded, the force of the discharge came in our direction and blew us through the door of the hotel into the bar," Murray said. "When we tried to return, the debris in the room, which we had just been blown from, was piled high and prevented our entrance. This also gave the police time to man the breach, and they opened fire with bombs and rifles. An attempt was made to set the roof alight, but, as we had not sufficient petrol to do this, we had to retire."[14]

Before he left, though, Murray nearly resorted to a desperate measure—gas warfare.

"I remember holding a bomb (German), which was believed to be a gas bomb, and wondering whether I should let it go or not," he later wrote. "Someone sensibly said, 'Do it if you want to gas us all.'"[15]

Having already nearly blown themselves up—Sandow Donovan's hat was shredded by the blast—Murray decided that gassing themselves would do little to advance the cause of Irish independence.

The attack was a tactical failure but a strategic success—the police abandoned the damaged building.

The smoke had scarcely cleared in Blarney before Murray was in on a rerun of the operation, this time in Cork city. On July 1, the rebels had a go at the King Street RIC Barracks, which was close to the seat of British power in the city, Victoria Barracks.

"The RIC barracks was situated near the military barracks, and it was felt that the attack would have to be quick," Murray said. "Guncotton was again used, and entrance gained into the house of Professor O'Donovan who lived alongside the barracks."[16]

The result was the same as in Blarney—the rebels didn't take the building, but it had to be abandoned.

To Kill a Colonel

The next mission in the war on the police was more successful and more spectacular—the assassination of Lieutenant Colonel Gerald Bryce Ferguson Smyth, divisional police commissioner for the province of Munster.

Smyth, who had lost an arm and won the Croix de Guerre in World War I, incurred the wrath of republicans when he urged the harshest possible measures to regain control of the countryside. He made the point during a June 17 meeting in Listowel, County Kerry, with some constables dispirited to the point of mutiny.

Smyth's solution to barracks attacks was simple. One constable, Jeremiah Mee, quoted him as saying: "If a police barracks is burned, or if the barracks already occupied is not suitable, then the best house in the locality is to be commandeered, the occupants thrown out in the gutter. Let him die there, the more the merrier."[17]

But that wasn't the worst of it, in Mee's telling:

> Police and military will patrol the country roads at least five nights a week. They are not to confine themselves to the main roads but take across country, lie in ambush, take cover behind fences, near the roads, and, when civilians are seen approaching, shout "hands up." Should the order be not immediately obeyed, shoot, and shoot with effect. If the persons approaching carry their hands in their pockets or are in any way suspicious looking, shoot them down. You may make mistakes occasionally and innocent persons may be shot, but this cannot be helped, and you are bound to get the right persons sometimes. The more you shoot, the better I will like you, and I assure you that no policeman will get into trouble for shooting any man.

Mee's account of exactly what Smyth said in the meeting has been disputed, but one thing is certain: The constable was having none of it.

"To hell with you, you are a murderer," he shouted, surprising Smyth and everyone else in the room. The lieutenant colonel promptly ordered his arrest. Calmer heads prevailed, and Mee and several others were allowed to resign. But Smyth moved to the top of the IRA's hit list.

Early in July 1920, Healy recalled, "the Brigade decided that an attempt should be made to shoot him." On July 17, exactly a month after the Listowel incident, the Cork brigade got word that Smyth was staying in the Cork County Club, "the resort of landed families and high military officers," as Healy put it.[18]

As Pa Murray and Martin Donovan stood guard outside, Danny Healy entered the club with Sandow Donovan and several other gunmen around 10 p.m.

"The six of us went into the County Club and down a passage to the lounge which we entered with drawn revolvers," Healy said. "Smyth was seated with another man—County Inspector Craig of the RIC—in a corner of the lounge in which there were about twelve other people. We immediately opened fire, killing Smyth and wounding Craig. Smyth tried to draw his revolver when he saw us entering the lounge but without avail."

Healy is a fairly reliable narrator, and if he says they immediately opened fire, they probably did. But there is a story that one of the gunmen had a few words for Smyth just before pulling the trigger: "Were not your orders to shoot at sight? Well, you are in sight now, so prepare."[19]

One key strategy in neutralizing the police was the elimination of their sources of information—informers and paid spies. No secret army can survive if its secrets are spilled to its enemies, and the Cork IRA was regarded as having an especially low bar for acting on any suspicions. Danny Healy executed at least one suspected informer. What neither Healy nor any of his IRA comrades knew was that there was a paid spy right in the midst of their C Company stronghold, Clogheen.

His name was Paddy O'Connor.

By this point, O'Connor had moved on from his job shoveling coal to working in the furniture section of Roches, a department store in central Cork. As he bicycled into and out of the city each day, he got into a feud with some unlikely opponents—Cork's working girls. "He had a kind of a persecution mania against prostitutes," said Stan Barry, an IRA man who lived in the area. The trees and shrubs along the Lee Road near O'Connor's home in Mount Desert provided cover for a multitude of sins, and sinners. One day one of the prostitutes haunting that area made the mistake of speaking to him.

"He was cycling in along the Lee Road opposite the quarry," Barry recalled. "'Good morning,' says one of the whores to him. He got off his bicycle, hit her in the face, then cycled away."

The payback wasn't long in coming—when O'Connor returned home along the same route later that day, three prostitutes ambushed him, gave him a good hiding, and raked his face with fingernails. And that wasn't the end of it. O'Connor later tangled with an aging prostitute who dared to address him.

We may never know exactly why O'Connor became a spy for the crown, but it seems that he was reporting to the constabulary—after he was shot in New York, his mother said he'd been a member of the RIC. It may be that he started his career as a tout by informing on prostitutes, enlisting the majesty of the law in his private vendetta, just as his family had done in their feud with the Deasys.

Or there could have been a political motivation. The O'Connors were politically active before the Irish revolution, most likely on behalf of Redmond's Irish Parliamentary Party, because Cruxy's father had a municipal job in a city dominated by machine politics and patronage. The 1918 electoral earthquake that elevated Sinn Fein smashed the traditional machine politics of Cork, leaving some supporters of the old order angry and embittered at the upstart republicans. Perhaps it was this—and the knowledge that members of the rival Deasy clan were active in the Volunteer movement—that led O'Connor to spy on the separatists.

Or maybe he simply needed money.

Whatever information he provided about the independence movement likely made its way to the British Army's intelligence chief in Cork, who was in close touch with the police. An Irishman with a distinguished record in World War I, he was one of the more colorful characters in the Irish War for Independence.

The Spymaster

The top British intelligence officer in Cork bore an odd resemblance to the Cruxy O'Connor of legend. He was a Catholic Irishman who joined the British Army, served in World War I, and won the Croix de Guerre as a sergeant in France. Cruxy was an Irish Catholic who was said to have joined the British Army, served in World War I, and won the Croix de Guerre as a sergeant major.

There was overlap, too, in their names: The spymaster was Campbell Joseph O'Connor Kelly. Cruxy's full name was Patrick Joseph O'Connor. They were the same age, born just a month apart in 1893. There were even rumors, however unlikely, that Kelly had succeeded in joining an IRA flying column in Cork, and taken part in operations against British forces, just as O'Connor would do.[20]

Lest anyone begin to suspect that O'Connor and Kelly were one and the same, it's clear that they were not. While Paddy O'Connor was in Cork, working on the railroad in 1911, Kelly was in the army, having lied about his age to enlist as a private at sixteen. He rose through the ranks and in 1918 he won the Military Cross for "conspicuous gallantry and devotion to duty" while serving with an artillery unit.[21]

The citation read: "While out with a patrol he encountered a strong hostile party, who bombed him, but by using his revolver he succeeded in getting away and bringing back information. Again, he did excellent work with a party of gunners, with rifles, in holding up the enemy while the guns were being withdrawn. He frequently returned to the battery under heavy fire to obtain further supplies of ammunition, though at the time he was suffering from the effects of gas."

In Cork, Kelly became an expert in the care and feeding of stool pigeons. On March 15, 1921—just days before O'Connor's arrest and the Ballycannon killings—he wrote a fellow officer about how to handle an informer he was planning to plant in cells with republican prisoners, whom Kelly called "Shinners":

"Do not put him with more than one Shinner at a time," Kelly advised, adding, "Do not keep the 'pigeon' too long on any one bird or he may get fed up. I will let you know later about his pay, food, etc. He must be kept in your barracks, or if taken out must be well disguised. It is better to take him out only at night."

The informer was Dan Shields, whom Kelly said had assisted "in the destruction of a few very much wanted members" of an elite IRA Active Service Unit. Shields had been disdained by his rebel comrades, and he got six of them killed as a result of an ambush at Mourne Abbey, likely because of the way they treated him.[22]

Kelly was born in the tiny County Mayo village of Knock in January 1893, just fourteen years after a religious sensation there—the sighting of the Virgin Mary and other religious figures on the outside wall of the local Catholic church. The church thus became a pilgrimage site, and Knock became synonymous with Irish miracles. It is a minor miracle that Kelly survived not just the Great War, but the War for Independence—Pa Murray said his death was a top priority for the IRA in Cork.

Kelly's movements were carefully monitored by his enemies, so a sojourn with a flying column seems a stretch, but he did have spies on his payroll, and that proved important in the summer of 1920.

After months of harrying the police, the Cork IRA decided in late July to turn its attention to the British Army. The poorly armed rebels needed weapons; the army had tons of guns. It was time to try to grab some from one of the military lorries moving about Cork. Reliable men were selected from a variety of units, Pa Murray among them. On the morning of August 2, they struck at White's Cross, north of the city. Murray said they took up positions behind a roadside fence at a right-angled bend in the road.

"One lorry came along, preceded by a motorcyclist. When the lorry came to an arranged spot, fire was opened on it, and the driver was killed. We expected that the car would run straight on to a ditch, where some of our party were placed, and that it would come under fire from men on the opposite side of the road."[23] But someone else in the lorry grabbed the wheel and negotiated the curve. Murray tossed a bomb, but the explosion didn't have the desired effect: "The soldiers opened fire with a machine gun. We were unable to lift our heads, and we retreated."

Ten days later, the army struck back, in a raid that would have stunning consequences.

On August 12, 1920, British troops stormed the city hall office of Terence MacSwiney, the lord mayor and commander of the Cork No. 1 Brigade. Captain Kelly, "the astute Intelligence officer of the British Sixth Division in Cork," as Florrie O'Donoghue put it, had gotten wind that the big fish were meeting, supposedly from a letter intercepted on August 9.[24] MacSwiney was hauled up in the net along with a shoal of top Cork IRA leaders, in what should have been the biggest British intelligence coup of the war in Cork.[25]

But it turned out to be a catch-and-release affair for the likes of MacSwiney's deputy commander, Sean O'Hegarty; Liam Lynch, the commander of the Cork No. 2 Brigade; Sandow Donovan, the leader of the 1st Battalion; and several others—the Army didn't seem to know who they had. But MacSwiney was a keeper. Within days he was court-martialed on charges of possessing seditious documents and police codes.

The court-martial was made possible by a new law called the Restoration of Order in Ireland Act (it would not live up to its billing).[26] Enacted just three days before the raid on city hall, it gave military courts jurisdiction over a wide range of crimes. MacSwiney refused to recognize the legitimacy of the proceedings.

Even before he was convicted and given a two-year sentence, he announced a desperate protest—a fast unto death. "I have taken no food since Thursday; therefore, I will be free within a month," he said. "I have decided the terms of my detention whatever your government may do. I shall be free, alive or dead, within a month."[27]

Thus opened a morality play of martyrdom that would reverberate from the streets of London to the docks of New York. It would end with Pa Murray and Martin Donovan heading off to assassinate the British cabinet.

Chapter 5

The Doomsday Plot

TERENCE MACSWINEY, LIKE Patrick Pearse before him, lived and died a zealous republican with a flair for drama. His day job as an accounting clerk left him unfulfilled; in 1899, at age 19, he helped found the Cork Celtic Literary Society.[1] In 1902, he protested a royal visit to Cork with a symbolic flourish, unfurling a large black flag from the window of the society's office as King Edward VII made his way down Great Georges Street.

MacSwiney's literary efforts told Cork everything it needed to know about his politics. His poems invoked the rebels of a century before. His first play focused on ancient Irish warriors, fighting to be free: "While still the fight undaunted you maintained. You kept men thinking of the ways of freedom."[2]

His last play, "The Revolutionist," was about an Irish rebel who wills his own death for the sake of the cause.[3] In short, the man had given a lot of thought to the business of mesmerizing an audience. And his last act would appear on a worldwide stage.

MacSwiney didn't invent the hunger strike. It was an ancient Irish means of redress for the aggrieved; William Butler Yeats wrote a play about it in 1904, "At the King's Threshold." Militant suffragettes introduced the tactic to the United Kingdom about six years later, and though none died in prison, the protests gained widespread publicity throughout Britain and Ireland.[4]

In September 1917, the hunger strike returned to Ireland. Thomas Ashe, a veteran of the Easter Rising, and several other republican prisoners stopped eating, demanding that they be treated as prisoners of war. Five days into the strike, Ashe died from pneumonia and forced feeding.[5] The case drew outrage across Ireland, and as Britain caved to the prisoners' demands, MacSwiney took note. On August 11, the day before MacSwiney's arrest, eleven republican prisoners in Cork resurrected the strategy, and the lord mayor soon joined them.

Within days, MacSwiney was winning international attention. In New York, an ad hoc corps of Irish American women versed in the confrontational tactics of the suffrage movement picketed the British consulate on August 23. They called themselves the "American Women Pickets for the Enforcement of America's War Aims" (self-determination for small nations).[6] And their signs pointedly referred to the killing of McCurtain, MacSwiney's predecessor: "Are two Mayors of Cork to be murdered in six months to sustain British rule in Ireland?"[7]

On day two of their protest, the women were doused with a bucket of water from the window of a US Navy office in the same building as the consulate. It was like pouring gasoline on a barbecue. A few days later, the women headed down to the Chelsea waterfront, where a British ship, the *Baltic* of the White Star Line, was docked. With an inspired bit of rabble-rousing—"Quit your jobs now, and we will tie up every British ship in this port"—they convinced hundreds of Irish American dockworkers to hit the bricks in support of MacSwiney.

This was not the first time the women had caused some righteous trouble on the New York waterfront, or on the *Baltic*, for that matter. Just a month before they literally led the charge at the Chelsea docks when Britain tried to ban Archbishop Daniel Mannix from boarding the Ireland-bound liner.

A native of Cork appointed to the Melbourne, Australia, archdiocese, Mannix had just conducted a tour of the United States on behalf of Irish independence. The British government wanted him in Ireland about as much as it wanted the plague in London. On July 30, when it was time for the archbishop to board the *Baltic*, thousands of Irish American New Yorkers showed up to escort him aboard, but a line of policemen barred the entrance to the pier. The women charged the police, with the crowd surging behind. Chaos ensued—when an English passenger heckled the crowd, Irish longshoremen loading the ship swarmed him, and Mannix himself had to restore order. The Battle of Pier 60 marked a decisive victory for the Irish, but the Royal Navy unceremoniously hauled the archbishop off the *Baltic* within sight of the Irish coast. His treatment only gave the women pickets another grievance when they returned to the docks, almost a month later, after the *Baltic* steamed back into port.[8]

British shipping was soon being boycotted up and down the Hudson, and not just by Irish longshoremen. Black dockers joined in, shouting "free Africa!" British imperialism had made lots of enemies, including Marcus Garvey, the black nationalist leader who carried clout with African Americans on the waterfront.[9]

By early September, the wildcat strike had spread to Boston and Brooklyn, where longshoremen demanded the release of MacSwiney and a British military withdrawal from Ireland.[10] "Three thousand stalwart men have stopped work to force the British Lion out of Brooklyn or British troops out of Ireland," declared an insurgent labor leader, Patrick McGovern. In Boston, fists flew when three less-than-stalwart dockworkers attempted to actually work on the docks. Badly outnumbered, they were quickly convinced that discretion was the better part of labor that day.

The strike wasn't called off until September 21. *The New York Sun* termed it "the first purely political strike of workingmen in the history of the United States," which seems an overstatement.[11]

Years later, Jimmy McGee, the IRA's waterfront fixer, claimed credit for the success and spread of the walkout, which also seems like an overstatement: "I also organized the strike on British ships by taking off the engine room force on the mail and passenger ships in the port of New York, which spread to Boston and Philadelphia, causing delay and trouble for the British shipping, which was considerable."[12]

Whatever aid McGee may have provided, the women pickets were clearly the driving force behind the walkout.

The strike wasn't the only American pressure. Mayor John Hylan of New York, the son of an immigrant from County Cavan, pleaded for MacSwiney's release, only to be rebuffed by Prime Minister Lloyd George.[13] Bonar Law, a top member of the British cabinet, had the same response to Britain's Labor Party. Even the king couldn't budge the cabinet. George V made clear that he feared the repercussions from MacSwiney's death more than those of his release from prison. The cabinet responded that "the release of the lord mayor would have disastrous results in Ireland and would probably lead to a mutiny of both military and police in the South of Ireland."[14] Seven years after portions of the British officer corps nearly mutinied over government policy in Ireland, London still felt constrained by the threat.

And so, London left Terence MacSwiney to die.

Cork No. 1 Brigade of the IRA wasn't about to do the same without trying something. The plan: a prisoner swap. The problem: They'd first have to capture a prisoner equal in worth to MacSwiney. The target: Lieutenant General Peter Strickland, the commander of the British Army's Sixth

Division in Cork.[15] Martin Donovan and several other reliable men were recruited for the Strickland abduction.[16]

The plan, while audacious, was not unprecedented. The North Cork brigade, under Liam Lynch, had snatched Brigadier General Cuthbert Lucas while he was fishing near Fermoy in late June. Shifted out of the county to foil the British search for him, the general later recounted that he convinced his IRA captors that he was entitled to a bottle of whiskey a day, and then proceeded to teach them a thing or two about the finer points of poker and other card games. With the cost of his booze and their poker lessons making his further confinement a losing proposition, the guards loosened security, and the general made good his escape.[17]

Strickland got away, too, but it was the kind of close shave that draws blood.

The plan called for snatching the general as he was driven to a Britain-bound ship. Michael Kenny, an IRA intelligence officer who recognized Strickland, would signal two brothers as the car came down Patrick's Hill. The brothers would jump on the running boards to commandeer the vehicle. Then the general and whoever was with him—which turned out to be the Sixth Division's intelligence chief, Captain Kelly—would be transferred to two waiting cars and removed to a safe house in the country.[18]

But signals were missed, and as the car whizzed by, Kenny opened fire with a pistol. Officers in the car shot back, and soon the other IRA men were blazing away. A wild gunfight left Strickland, sitting in the back, wounded in the shoulder. Right next to him, Kelly got an up-close and personal look at what an intelligence failure looks like. The bullet-riddled vehicle accelerated away, taking with it Terence MacSwiney's last chance of survival.

Starvation is an ugly way to go, and just seventy years after the trauma of the potato famine, which cost a million lives, it held a particular emotional resonance in Ireland. Only the most self-disciplined can carry the act through to its awful conclusion. MacSwiney was steeled in his determination by his shame over Cork's failure in the Easter Uprising when he arrived at Beal na Blath with orders for the Volunteers to stand down. Two months after that he wrote:

Because I have endured the pain
Of waiting, while my comrades died
Let me be swept in war's red rain,
And friends and foes be justified.[19]

In 1920, weeks without food did nothing to change his mind. On September 30, some thirty-nine days into his hunger strike, he wrote to his friend Cathal Brugha, the rebel government's minister for defense: "If I die, I know the fruit will exceed the cost a thousand-fold. The thought makes me happy. I thank God for it. Ah, Cathal, the pain of Easter Week is properly dead at last."[20]

Many factors help explain why the revolutionary flame burned hottest in Cork, but the blushing shame of Beal na Blath certainly ranks near the top of the factors that made the violence there unique.

By the end of August, the IRA foresaw the eventual, awful outcome, and was planning a spectacular act of retribution. There would be hell to pay for the second consecutive death of a lord mayor of Cork. After the first, the bill landed in the lap of a few policemen, despite the coroner jury's verdict blaming the British cabinet. After the second, the cabinet would be made to pay, in a sort of doomsday plot. Among the bill collectors: Pa Murray, Martin Donovan, and Tommy Dennehy, all of C Company, 1st Battalion, Cork No. 1 Brigade of the Irish Republican Army. Dennehy would be among the six men killed when O'Connor decided to talk.

Murray was an advance scout for the assassination project.

In late August, Sandow Donovan, the commander of the 1st Battalion, asked Murray if he would go to London to take care of a special job for Michael Collins, the preeminent revolutionary who served as minister of finance for the republican government and director of intelligence for the IRA. Murray agreed and met with Collins in Dublin. "He explained that, if Terence MacSwiney died on hunger strike, it had been decided to shoot some members of the British cabinet," Murray said. "He gave me a number of names, which I had to memorize at the time, and left full discretion to me as to what should be done."[21]

Collins warned Murray that it might be a one-way trip: He "could hold out no hope that myself or any man taking part in the action would be rescued." And he made one point crystal clear: "Under no circumstances was anything to be attempted before Terence MacSwiney died."

Murray headed to England that night, accompanied by Jack Cody as wheelman. In London, he got in touch with Sam Maguire, the IRA's intelligence chief in Britain. Maguire arranged digs for Murray and Cody and made financial arrangements for the mission. After an inspection of the rebel contingent in London, Murray picked a select group to help determine the habits of the cabinet ministers. He also touched base with Irish newspapermen, who provided background information on the targets.

During the next six weeks of surveillance, Murray said, "I acquainted myself with the streets where these ministers were living, and the routes they might possibly take to and from the House of Commons. Cody, who was to drive a car, was also familiarizing himself with London conditions."

But to Murray's consternation, the ministers were varying their routes, and he couldn't come up with a definite plan. Collins nonetheless sent word that he wanted some kind of assassination attempted should MacSwiney die. By mid-October, the outcome seemed clear, and Murray found the purgatory of awaiting a suicide mission to be excruciating: "The strain of the last six or eight weeks was very severe," he wrote. "We were coming to the stage where anything might happen to ourselves or in the work we had undertaken."

The strain may explain Murray's rash decision, when an opportunity arose, to ignore his orders and strike before MacSwiney died. He had his sights trained on no less a figure than Lord Balfour, the former prime minister who was serving in the cabinet as lord president of the council.

"I was informed that Balfour would be going to Oxford on a Tuesday, about mid-October, and I immediately sent word to Collins that, whether Terence MacSwiney was dead or alive then, we would attempt to shoot Balfour. I sent word on a Sunday night, and the courier returned on Monday recalling myself and the other as, for some reason or other, Collins did not wish this operation to be carried out."[22]

Murray followed the order, but he had to prove to himself that he could have pulled off the job.

"I went to Oxford on the appointed day and met and spoke to Mr. Balfour on the street," he said. "I simply walked up to him and asked him the way to some of the Oxford colleges. He directed me and said, 'You are an Irishman?' I said, 'Yes,' and he walked a bit of the way with me. He did not appear to have an armed guard with him."

When Murray returned to Dublin, Collins told him he was sorry, but that they could not do anything until MacSwiney died. Cathal Brugha, another top official in the rebel government, told him the mission should never have been conceived, and could only be executed by accident, as might have happened in Oxford.

The proof of that came from Sean Flood, a Dublin IRA man who apparently came closest to harming a cabinet member in the doomsday plot. In a high-spirited race through the Westminster tube station, he rounded a corner and, quite by accident, slammed straight into Lloyd George. The prime minister had a couple of detectives at his side, and Flood nearly got himself shot before George told his guards to take their gunsights off a man who was actively plotting his assassination.[23]

Murray was the brains of the operation, but he needed good triggermen, and a couple of guys from his C Company fit the bill. One was Tommy

Dennehy.[24] The other, unsurprisingly, was Martin Donovan. After the Strickland ambush, Donovan headed up to Dublin with a couple of other picked men, Stephen Foley and Sean Healy. They took a train from Blarney, to avoid the British spies haunting the Cork station.

As the train left, they were in high spirits, three comrades "with no cares or worries," as Healy put it, belting out "Blarney Roses"—"Can anybody tell me where the Blarney roses grow?"[25] Then they sang a parody based on a more recent mystery: "Can anybody tell where did General Lucas go?" (He'd been kidnapped.) They acted more like they were heading off on holiday instead of marching straight into the teeth of the most audacious assault on the government in London since Guy Fawkes and the Gunpowder Plot.

The men, from different IRA units, didn't know each other until they met at the train, but they quickly realized they'd all been in on the Blarney Barracks attack, and "a fast and endurable friendship was at once formed," Healy said. Foley kept them entertained with a story of his exploits that night in Blarney. In the chaos after the explosion that blew Murray into the barroom, Foley had clambered onto the barracks roof with a can of gasoline, planning to break a hole in the slates, pour in the gas, and set the place alight. He broke a hole through the roof, all right—the slates, perhaps weakened by the blast, gave way beneath his feet. Foley plunged into a room filled with blinding clouds of smoke and dust from the blast—and was immediately pounced on by two men. He suspected the worst of them, they suspected the worst of him, and a tussle ensued.

"Not knowing whether he fell into the police barrack or the hotel, he was of the opinion that the men who held him were RIC men, and they, in turn, thought they had captured an RIC man. When they all recognized each other, they had the heartiest laugh of their lives."

Martin Donovan then regaled his companions with his tale of the Mac-Neilus prison breakout, calling it "the most thrilling experience of his life."

As the train rolled closer to Dublin, the mood darkened. They talked of the torture inflicted on rebels by crown forces—of Tom Hales, the Bandon commander, his fingernails crushed, one by one. Of men pricked with bayonets or put up against walls with loaded guns to their foreheads and given a slow count to ten to divulge names. "We were wondering if we would have the courage to stand up to such treatment," Healy said.[26]

When they got to Dublin they checked into Vaughan's Hotel, a favored haunt of republicans. Mick Collins and Cathal Brugha—the heart of the rebel government while de Valera was off raising money in America—met with them that night.

Collins was light and breezy, buying them each a Guinness. If the Cork city IRA commander Sean O'Hegarty had recruited them for the job, Collins joked, their "guns must be well-notched." Brugha was dark and serious. It was "war to the knife" for both sides now, he told the men, emphasizing the dangers that lay ahead, for them and the movement. "The plot to kill the prime minister of England, if brought to fruition, might have worldwide repercussions," he said.[27]

A few days later, Collins met again with Donovan, Healy, and Foley. The mission was off. Lloyd George was making noises about a truce. It was best not to mow down the prime minister and the British cabinet. Not just yet anyhow.

Donovan headed back to Cork, where he was promptly lifted by the authorities and imprisoned until May 1921.[28] As Donovan went off to prison, the hunger strikes were reaching their climax. The first to die, in Cork on October 17, was Michael Fitzgerald.[29] On October 25, two more died— Joseph Murphy in Cork and Terence MacSwiney in London.

With MacSwiney's long-feared death, protests swept the trans-Atlantic world. In New York, five thousand protesters gathered in Columbus Circle. When one attendee, thirty-year-old Joseph Dugan, offered some unkind words about a poetry-spouting speaker, his "to hell with him" remark was misinterpreted as a reference to the lord mayor, and he nearly ended up as dead as MacSwiney.[30] Pummeled by a mob, Dugan had to be rescued by a patrolman with a drawn revolver. In November, as thousands of mourners filed out of a memorial service for MacSwiney at St. Patrick's Cathedral on Fifth Avenue, the nearby Union League came under attack because it was displaying a British flag.[31]

And it wasn't just New York. Belfast erupted, Barcelona rioted, and a bombing was foiled in Buenos Aires.[32] Even Londoners lined the streets to pay their silent respects as MacSwiney's body was moved from Brixton prison. When it arrived back in Cork, the city staged a mass funeral for the lord mayor.

While cooler heads had prevailed on the issue of massacring the British cabinet—MacSwiney's martyrdom was not to be besmirched with the blood of the high and mighty—the Cork IRA did launch a major offensive against the British intelligence operation that had effected his arrest. Within weeks, six military officers and five civilians thought to be involved in spying were executed by the Cork No. 1 Brigade, aided by a strategically placed mole in the heart of British intelligence in Victoria Barracks.[33]

Danny Healy, as usual, was in on the action. On November 21, he attempted to kidnap a British officer, possibly Captain Kelly, only to fall victim to a rare bit of bad intelligence.

"Late in the month of November 1920, we received information from our intelligence service that a senior military Intelligence officer would attend Mass on a certain Sunday in St. Patrick's Church, Glanmire, Cork, accompanied by an intelligence officer from Cork Barracks," he said. "We were instructed to kidnap this officer and hand him over to the brigade."[34]

With four other rebels, he waited outside the church until the service ended. "After Mass we saw Constable Carroll and his companion leaving with the crowd of people," he said. "We held up both of them with revolvers and then released Carroll, taking away by motor the other man who, we thought, was the military intelligence officer. It subsequently transpired that the man we had taken away was a Constable Ryan and not the person we sought. Ryan was later released unharmed."

Healy came up short, but in Dublin that day, the IRA pulled off a stunning series of coordinated attacks on British intelligence officers. By the end of the day, a dozen of the undercover agents were dead, and in retaliation, rampaging police opened fire without warning at a Gaelic football match in Croke Park, killing fourteen civilians, including players and children.

They called it Bloody Sunday.

A week later, the IRA hammered British forces again, this time in West Cork. On November 28, a column commanded by Tom Barry wiped out an Auxiliary patrol at Kilmichael. Only one of the eighteen policemen survived the ambush, compared to three deaths for the insurgents.

In early December, Healy and Pa Murray went gunning for the biggest intelligence prize in Cork city: Captain Kelly. The captain was married, but he had an eye for the ladies, so the boys of C Company tried one of the oldest tricks in the book. "Several unsuccessful attempts were made to get him, including the charms of [a] young lady to get him away from the vicinity of the barracks," P. J. Murphy said. Along with Murray, Healy, Mick Bowles, and two others, he lay in wait for four nights. The canny Kelly never showed.[35]

The wave of attacks prompted a public warning by British forces that they would assassinate republicans and destroy private property if the violence continued.[36] On December 10, the authorities imposed martial law. Anyone caught with a gun faced a firing squad, and civilians were cautioned that their homes could be destroyed if they failed to warn about an impending attack on crown forces.

The very next day, the rebels struck again, and Cork descended into hell.

The attack targeted Captain Kelly, the British spymaster.[37] IRA intelligence reported that Kelly would accompany two trucks loaded with about twelve Auxiliaries each. At Dillons Cross, near Victoria Barracks, Michael Kenny—the same man who had played a central role in the attempt to kidnap General Strickland—stepped into the street, raised his hand and blew a whistle as the convoy approached. When the lorries slowed, five IRA men hidden behind a wall heaved hand grenades. The explosions killed one Auxiliary and wounded twelve more, but Kelly was not among them.[38] The apoplectic comrades of the dead and wounded unleashed an orgy of arson and looting that would reverberate around the world.

Soon, much of central Cork was ablaze.

At the Shamrock Hotel, Michael V. O'Donoghue watched as the flames spread. He left a detailed account of the unfolding terror:

> Billows of red flame roared and swelled high in the air about 200 yards northeast of us. As far as we could discern, Patrick Street south from Winthrop Street to Princes Street was one huge inferno blazing, roaring and crackling. There was little smoke. The sky was clear and starry, the air was still and dry, as it was freezing. As we watched the devouring flames, awe-struck and fascinated, our backs and bodies generally shivered in the cold frosty air of the roof; but, turning our faces to the red-roaring holocaust, we felt the heatwaves beating against our faces. It was an extraordinary experience.[39]

Wondering if the flames would keep heading toward him, he noticed that the fire had opened a second front:

> Now a great new conflagration, about 1,000 yards southeast of us attracts our attention. It is the city hall on the south side of the Lee, less than 200 yards from the great RIC headquarters in Union Quay. The two huge fires blaze and billow to the heavens as if each was endeavouring to excel the other in ferocity and in spectacular intensity.

Neither O'Donoghue nor his companions got any sleep that night. Drunken Auxiliaries were shooting at firefighters and cutting their hoses.[40] When the sun rose, a hundred businesses were destroyed or damaged, and city hall was a ruin. The British blamed the IRA, but almost no one was fooled, and almost everyone was outraged.

There's no surer sign that the cause is lost than when government forces start destroying the places they're supposed to hold for the government. At least one British sympathizer had already switched sides as Cork combed through the rubble.

Paddy O'Connor had joined the IRA. And with his workplace in ashes— the flames had devoured Roches Stores—he had plenty of time to devote to the cause.

Exactly when O'Connor stopped spying for the British is uncertain, but it was probably before the fall of 1919. Were he still working for the crown after that, the IRA mole in Kelly's office would have been in a good position to know, and he might have met the same fate as the other five civilians killed as spies in November.

While the rest of the IRA was waging war on the British, O'Connor was pressing his feud with the prostitutes along the Lee Road—and he got the Cork city brigade involved.

Stan Barry, an IRA comrade, recalled that O'Connor convinced brigade headquarters to order a roundup of the working girls. It appears that O'Connor may have had some pull with the commander of the Cork city brigade— another IRA man described him as O'Hegarty's fair-haired boy.[41]

Following orders, Barry commandeered a vehicle, collected O'Connor, and started rounding up the suspected prostitutes. "I got five or six of them in a van and I had Conners and another fellow with me," he said. "We brought them up to the Good Shepherd Convent and there we handed them over to the nuns. I behaved like a perfect gentleman that day, but Conners was all for beating them."[42]

The women may have escaped O'Connor's fists, but they faced a different kind of hell. The Good Shepherd Convent amounted to a prison workhouse for unwed mothers, women suspected of prostitution, and girls with intellectual disabilities.[43]

In time, O'Connor moved from attacks on prostitutes to more lethal activities—he executed a suspected spy. "A spy was brought from the city by men from another area and was shot by P. Connors and Chris McSweeny," a unit activity report for December 1920 states.[44]

O'Connor may have been picked for the assignment because of his familiarity with the quarry on Lee Road, which the IRA sometimes used as an execution site. Five months later, on May 20, 1921, a squad of rebels marched three captives into the quarry and shot them. Two—Edward Hawkins and John Sherlock—were former British soldiers; the third was Hawkins's father, Daniel. Amazingly, the elder Hawkins and Sherlock survived.[45]

O'Connor's first killing involved a man suspected of exactly the same offense that O'Connor had once committed. If you are going to embark on the awful business of killing human beings, there is probably no worse way to start than with a helpless civilian prisoner—one in some ways very much like yourself.

Chapter 6

The Coolavokig Ambush

O'CONNOR HAD PROVEN himself a gunman; now the IRA handed him the most lethal weapon in its arsenal: a machine gun. Specifically, a light Lewis gun—the kind used in World War I dogfights.

Michael Murphy, commander of the 2nd Battalion, had picked it up along with another Lewis gun and plenty of ammo at a second-hand gun shop in London in December and shipped them home in two barrels, via the Cork Steamship Company.[1] They were addressed to a non-existent firm, Messrs. Swanton & Company, North Main Street, Cork, and Murphy enlisted a reliable buddy, Sean Murphy, who worked as a clerk for Cork Steamship, to look after them when they arrived.

Murphy's law hadn't yet been conceived, but whatever could go wrong did.

When the shipment escaped the notice of Murphy's man at Cork Steamship, it was promptly dispatched to the non-existent address. When no Messrs. Swanton & Company could be found on North Main Street, it was promptly returned to the Cork Steamship Company. When a curious employee pried open one of the barrels, he promptly called the police.

By this point, the dire nature of the situation had dawned on the steamship clerk, and he tipped off Michael Murphy, who grabbed a gun and dashed to the warehouse with a cart.

"Producing the revolver, I ordered the barrel to be loaded onto the cart and made a hurried departure with my precious cargo," he recalled. "On my way back, I passed a party of detectives from Union Quay Barracks who were en route to the store to collect the stuff, but 'the bird had flown.'"[2]

The detectives at Union Quay quickly had reason to regret their late arrival. On January 4, 1921, one of the Lewis guns was turned against a patrol of ten officers right outside the barracks, with devastating effect.

Paddy O'Connor played a role in the attack. The Lewis gun had been stashed at the arms dump in Clogheen, so O'Connor and Mick Bowles brought the gun to the ambush, which was arranged by the 2nd Battalion.[3] Michael Murphy, its commander, described the action:

"At approximately 6:15 p.m. the police and Tans came out of Union Quay Barracks and, by the time they were ready to move, we fixed the Lewis gun in position on the roadway outside Moore's Hotel. As the enemy party proceeded towards Parnell Bridge, we opened fire with the Lewis gun."[4]

Other IRA men on the bridge attacked with grenades and pistols—all ten officers went down, two of them fatally wounded.[5]

Nine days later, O'Connor had a close scrape involving that same Lewis gun.

On January 13, the army and the Black and Tans, armed with inside information, raided the arms depot at the Bowles farm in Clogheen, close to the mental asylum. The arms cache included the Lewis gun. Sandow Donovan, Pa Murray, O'Connor, Deasy, and Mullane had spent the night before in a farm outbuilding, as did several other local boys from C Company—Willie Deasy's brother Jeremiah, Tom Dennehy, Dan Murphy, Mick O'Sullivan, and Dan Crowley. (Five of them wouldn't live to see the summer.)

Sentries were posted, and P. J. Murphy took the last watch, from 5 a.m. to 7 a.m. When the sun rose, many of the boys moved out—some had jobs to report to in the city. Among those remaining behind were Murphy, O'Connor, and Mick Bowles—they brought the Lewis gun and other arms to Bowles's house to show them off to Liam Deasy, a rebel commander from West Cork. "We were proud of its possession," Murphy said.[6] At 11 a.m. they were all having a cup of tea when they heard strange voices outside—crown forces were surrounding the place. "We picked up our equipment and made our escape," Murphy said. But a lot of weapons, including the machine gun, were left behind.

Into the breach stepped Mick Bowles's fifteen-year-old sister, Mary. The machine gun was lying near a fence, covered with a sheet. She donned a suit of body armor and grabbed the Lewis gun, which she stashed under her coat. Then, just for extra measure, she snatched two pistols and twenty-five rounds of ammunition and thus burdened, started to make her way

across the fields to return them to the IRA. It wasn't her first such mission—
she'd used a horse and cart to deliver the guns for the ambush the previous
summer that had killed Sergeant Denis Garvey and Constable Daniel
Harrington. She could have used the cart this time around. When the Lewis
gun slipped out from under her coat, the Black and Tans became just a little
suspicious.

Arrested and interrogated in Cork, young Mary wouldn't talk. Hauled
before a military tribunal, she refused to recognize the legitimacy of the
court and stood mute during the proceedings. When word spread that she
was being tortured, the Bishop of Cork intervened on her behalf. She thereby
became a legend in Cork, a sung hero:

> Mary Bowles the pride of sweet Clogheen
> Never yet was there known a maid a lady or a queen
> To match the deeds of Mary Bowles, the pride of sweet Clogheen
> And when dump was emptying out sure, Mary wasn't slow
> To hide the precious guns, she bravely tried to go.[7]

While crown forces were arresting Mary, O'Connor and his comrades
made good their escape—and there was only one place for him to go. By
now the British knew that O'Connor, the onetime spy, had gone over to the
IRA—the Black and Tans were raiding the O'Connor home in Mount Desert
on a regular basis, looking for him. And being Black and Tans, they took out
their frustration at not finding him by smashing the furniture and scaring
the hell out of his family. "We were in fear of our lives all the time," his
mother said. "We didn't know what time we would be shot. The Black and
Tans at each visit insisted we were harboring Patrick although we hadn't
seen him for months at a time. He was 'on the run' all the time with other
boys in the brigade, most of whom belonged in the vicinity of our home."[8]

The IRA had so many men on the run by the latter half of 1920 that it
hit upon a strategy that would become a nightmare for crown forces. By
grouping the best of the fugitives together and training them in "flying
columns," the IRA created full-time units that roamed the countryside,
living off the land and lying in wait to ambush the Black and Tans.

In the first weeks of 1921, O'Connor's brigade, the Cork No. 1, formed
its flying column. Along with about forty-five Volunteers from outlying rural
areas, he was among the handpicked few from Cork city: "sixteen of the best
and most highly skilled Volunteers," as one veteran put it.[9] Among the others
were Willie Deasy and Jerry Mullane, both members of C Company.

Sandow Donovan was in charge of the column, though Sean O'Hegarty,
the commander of the city brigade, went along, too. Pa Murray was the

adjutant and Sean Murray, O'Connor's childhood friend from Clogheen, was the drillmaster—he had served in the Great War with the Irish Guards. And so, after the raid on the Bowles farm, there was only one place for them to go—to the village of Ballyvourney for a rendezvous with the rest of the men who would make up the flying column. O'Connor was clearly a trusted member of the unit.

But that doesn't mean his comrades weren't above a little teasing.

It may have been en route to Ballyvourney that O'Connor ended up with his enduring nickname: Cruxy. According to one story, O'Connor earned the moniker as a decorated veteran of World War I. "He had been a sergeant-major in the British Army and we called him 'Cruxy' because he won some medal called the Croix de Guerre in France," said Sandow Donovan.[10]

There are a few problems with that story. For one, there is no documentation that O'Connor ever served in the British military or won the Croix de Guerre. For another, four comrades from C Company—Danny Healy, Jeremiah Deasy, Stan Barry, and Sean Murray—wrote accounts of O'Connor that offered no mention of him being in the military, and Murray was himself a British Army veteran. Finally, O'Connor's family says he never served in World War I.[11]

So whence the nickname?

Two sources say it arose from mockery of O'Connor's bad French. According to one account, "On the way out to Ballyvourney from Cork City, the young machine-gunner had boasted that he meant to earn the 'Croix de Guerre,' the French supreme military honor, which had been so frequently in the news during the war years. His comrades just as airily corrupted his inept French and hung on him the label 'Crux na Gurra,' and so he stayed."[12]

A similar story was told by a Cork resident who in the 1960s had extensive dealing with IRA veterans of the flying column who served with O'Connor. He said O'Connor got the name because he was reading a newspaper and remarked on a story about someone who had received the Croix de Guerre—mispronouncing it as "Crox."[13] Neither the boast nor the mangled pronunciation seems like the sort of thing that would come out of the mouth of a British Army sergeant major who had spent years fighting in France.

When the column formed in Ballyvourney, O'Connor faced suspicion and hostility from the column's rural contingent, in addition to the mockery from the city men. Some of the country boys found O'Connor to be a bit too curious. Mick O'Sullivan, who manned the column's other Lewis gun, said O'Connor was "overly inquisitive about the names of people and places while with the column."[14] Maybe he was just a city boy in the country, getting acquainted with new comrades and a new landscape. But questions galore were a recipe for suspicion among rebels on the run in a land long plagued by informers.

Stan Barry, a column member who worked closely with Cruxy, put it bluntly. "Conners was unpopular" he said. "He had a bad temper." It didn't help matters when he was granted permission to leave the column to attend a christening. "This was a great joke with the column, and some very caustic comments were made," Barry recalled.[15]

And his habit of daily scribbling didn't help. "He kept a diary, and he wrote it up every night while he was in the Column," Sean Murray recalled—a practice that was to make more than a few comrades nervous in the months to come.[16]

Certainly, there were some differences between the Cork city men and the country boys in the column. The latter grew up on farms and were used to working the fields in the cold rain and gusting winds that made life a misery for the city fellows as they marched through the rural townlands and bedded down in unheated billets. The decision to entrust O'Connor with one of the column's Lewis guns did nothing to diminish the hostility of others in the column, some of whom had repaired it. "There had been screws and joints missing," Mick O'Sullivan complained. "But Jim Grey and I made them. And Conners got the gun." Sullivan felt the gun "should have gone to Jim Grey, who was a far better man. We were suspicious of Connors then."[17]

The new machine gun acquired a name all its own: "Bás gan sagart." It was an old Irish curse: death without a priest (to you). They called it "Bás" for short, as in "Give me the Bás."[18] It had somehow been gotten out of the British Army's Ballincollig Barracks near Cork city.[19]

Before taking the field, the column went through a sort of basic training at a farm outside Ballyvourney. The quarters proved a good introduction to the hardships they would face in the field—"an old, disused cow house with a leaking roof; it was cold and damp, with broken doors and windows." As the January winds blew, the men slept on straw, with more straw jammed around the doors and windows, "to keep out the cold winter frosts."[20]

There were no complaints about the food, though. This was farm country, and the locals were generous—"home-made bread, buckets of milk, bacon and eggs." And mutton, lots and lots of mutton. "Every morning one of our men went up the mountains and seized a sheep which was killed to provide dinner," Patrick Lynch said.[21]

The men rose at 6 a.m. for two hours of physical exercise, followed by drill in the use of rifle, bayonet, and hand grenades. This went on for two weeks, and then the men marched to Gougane Barra near the Kerry County line, for another ten days of training. By the time they finished, the IRA was ready to field a column of sixty men who were, for security purposes, constantly on the move.

It was time to go to war. It was time to go to Coolavokig.

The ambush site was nearly perfect. It lay at a small crossroads on the Macroom-Killarney Road, in an area referred to variously as Coolavokig, Paulnabro, and Coolnacaheragh. The main IRA position lay north of the road, where the Cork No. 1 Brigade's flying column occupied rocky ground that climbed sharply from the road. A smaller contingent from the 7th Battalion's flying column took positions on the south side. The British convoy would be approaching from the east. Charles Browne, who took part in the ambush, sketched out a rough map.

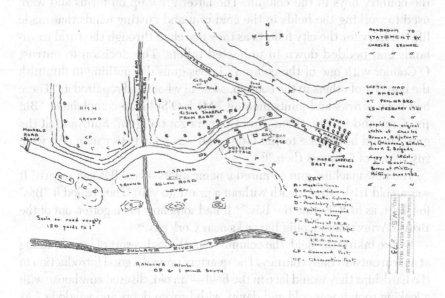

The machine guns, marked A, were placed at either end of the ambush site—steel jaws that would snap shut on the convoy, pinning the crown forces in place while IRA riflemen strung along the road raked them with withering volleys. O'Connor was given the crucial job of manning the Lewis gun at the east end of the ambush.

A roadblock was placed at the western end of the trap, to ensure the Tans didn't force their way through. The only real drawbacks to the site were two cottages on the south side of the road that had the potential to offer a haven from the lethal hell the ambushers were planning to unleash. The plan was sound enough, but it almost didn't work. The enemy wasn't cooperating.

Sixty IRA men were in place and raring to have a go at the Auxiliaries by 9 a.m., Friday, February 19, which was when a British convoy of eight vehicles with about eighty men normally moved down the road. But the enemy failed to show that day, or in the days that followed, as the men spent hours lying in the cold rain, sleet, and biting winds. At night they went back to their base miles away, disappointed, dispirited, and suffering from exposure. Morale sank. The men muttered. Even some officers urged that the whole operation be canceled. The city men were in bad shape—Pa Murray dropped out for health reasons.[22]

"I was suffering from blood poisoning," he said. "The doctor took me away to fix me up."[23]

Sean O'Hegarty, the gruff commanding officer of the Cork No. 1 Brigade, gave his discouraged officers a pep talk. "We came here to do a job, and we will do that job. We all agreed that it is either us or the Auxies," he said. "They are burning and looting worse than ever. We cannot go into Macroom to take them on. We would be cut to ribbons. Here is where we stay. Here is where we meet them."[24]

"Tomorrow is their usual day for raiding this area," he added. "Wait and see if they will come tomorrow."

Then, it appears, O'Hegarty and the commander of the column, Sandow Donovan, took a reckless gamble to ensure the enemy did come the next day. "Sean Hegarty and Dan Donovan (Sando) conceived the idea of sending a man into Macroom to let the enemy know we were waiting for them," recalled Dan Harrington, a Ballyvourney Volunteer.[25] "They selected an IRA man named Collins who had a brother killed in France fighting with the British forces. When Collins reached Macroom he had a couple of drinks and feigned drunkenness, while he let the military and Tans know that the IRA were located at Coolnacaheragh and were waiting for them."

The Tans rose to the bait the next morning, on February 25. They moved in cautiously, led by Major James Seafield Grant, a cool-headed young officer who'd been wounded in France and won the Military Cross. He'd been in Ireland for only three days.[26] The British arrived an hour earlier than usual, and they had one other nasty surprise for the IRA. As the convoy slowed to a snail's pace entering the kill zone, the British forced four civilian hostages to walk in front.

What came next was a confused melee, and the fact that many recollections of it were recorded decades later only adds another layer of fog to the battle. What seems clear is that days of waiting had made the ambushers careless—the early arrival of the Auxiliaries and their use of hostages threw the insurgents off guard.

One ambusher—Sandow Donovan would later claim it was O'Connor—had slipped unobserved across the road, and, out of position, tried to dash back as he heard the lorries approach. But that wasn't the only problem. Sean Murray, the drill instructor, said O'Connor was "just in the position we wanted him to be in to fire." But O'Connor and another man, O'Brien, "were working in their shirt sleeves, and you could see them miles away."[27]

The convoy spotted the suspicious activity and ground to a halt, opening fire. Still, the rebels held back, hoping the convoy would move further into the ambush zone. But that changed quickly when some Auxiliaries climbed off the lorries. They didn't get very far.

"A couple of them sent up into the rocky hillside to act as scouts were shot dead and immediately the fight was on," said Patrick O'Sullivan, an IRA officer on the scene. The hostages and many of the Auxiliaries dashed for cover in the cottages on the south side of the road.

O'Connor's Lewis gun let off a burst—some felt prematurely, because the convoy had not fully entered the killing zone. Mick O'Sullivan, another IRA machine-gunner who was there that day, said "Conners fired a shot, so it was he who gave the game away."[28]

But soon the Lewis gun wasn't firing at all. O'Connor said it jammed, and Mick O'Sullivan suggested that some clumsiness may have been involved: "That gun was dropped on the rock." Others, in retrospect, suspected darker reasons, but fear of hitting the hostages may have been a factor. At the western end of the ambush, the second machine gun stopped firing, too, for exactly that reason. All along the line, IRA gunfire slackened.

"The presence of the hostages jumbled up with the Auxiliaries in the mad scramble for cover had a disturbing effect on the fire of the attackers," Charles Browne recalled.[29]

It may have slackened, but the gunfire didn't end—rebel riflemen picked off several Auxiliaries as they ran to the cottages. Trying to restore order in all this madness was the Auxiliaries' commander, Major Grant. He was standing calmly in the road, surveying the situation through his binoculars, when a bullet killed his driver. Still, Grant stood his ground, trying to get the lay of the land.

"Jesus Christ. That bastard must be born lucky," one of the IRA gunners commented.[30] Then a bullet ripped through the major's heart.

One of the British cars backed up and headed for reinforcements—a move that deeply frustrated some ambushers who felt that O'Connor ought to have put it out of commission. "This car could have been shot to pieces by one of our machine gunners, who had it covered all the time, but he failed to open fire, whether for fear of the eight lorries of 'Tans' in front of him or not, we could never understand," said Patrick Lynch.[31]

In the chaos of the fighting, there was plenty of movement. Stan Barry, who was commanding O'Connor's section, said one of his men fled at the very start of the engagement, and others apparently followed. "Half your fellows ran away," O'Hegarty complained to Sean Murray, referring to the Cork city men. In the meantime, some rebels from the inactive western end of the ambush zone moved closer to the scene of the fighting.

The battle went on for hours, with the Auxiliaries falling back on the two cottages. The westernmost of the two was the most vulnerable, and as the IRA poured fire into it, the Tans' will to fight crumbled. "After some time, the enemy resistance seemed to weaken and return fire finally ceased," Charles Browne said. Just when it appeared the occupants were about to surrender, hundreds of British reinforcements began to arrive.

It was time to get out of Coolavokig.

Several rear-guard skirmishes broke out as the British tried to encircle the withdrawing IRA. Patrick O'Sullivan's unit got into a running fight around 2 p.m. but pulled through without any casualties. That evening, Patrick Lynch and nine others from the flying column were sitting down to a meal when they were alerted to approaching lorries. In a fighting withdrawal, one man, Patrick Casey, was wounded and captured.

By the time dawn broke the next day, the whole world knew that something big had happened in Coolavokig. "SINN FEIN FORCES IN BIGGEST FIGHT" read a front-page headline in the *New York Times*. English newspapers reported six dead among the crown forces. Some IRA men suggested the real number was much higher. Charles Browne put it at seven to fourteen.[32] Daniel Harrington claimed that "after nightfall at least thirty corpses were shipped in coffins from the quays in Cork City back to England."

The IRA had lost not a man in the actual ambush, but there was a sense that the column had not made the most of an opportunity to deal the British an even bigger blow—and grab some machinery from the enemy: "We were bitterly disappointed to leave such a prize of guns and ammunition behind."[33] The disappointment turned to recrimination as the column retreated toward Kerry. Those who hadn't measured up were called to account at a meeting.

"When they were all assembled Sean Hegarty had there before the table all the lads who were away from their positions and he sent some of them back to the city," Sean Murray recalled. "Mullane and Deasy went back. They were Ballycannon men, as was Connors."[34]

And they may not have been the only ones sent back. One rebel commander who served in the column recalled, "Out of a number of Volunteers sent from Cork City, we only retained about six."[35]

In the ranks, there was much grumbling about Cruxy O'Connor and the silent Lewis gun. What good was a gunman who stopped shooting? "He abandoned his gun and cleared off and it would have been lost had not a young lad named Dick Kingston picked it up," Mick O'Sullivan complained.[36] Sandow Donovan, the column commander, went much further, blaming O'Connor for pretty much everything that went wrong that day:

"I saw 'Cruxy' Connor run across the road from the cottage to the No. 1 Lewis gun post," he said. "He was one of the city men, from the Blarney Street Company, and was the No. 1 Lewis gunner. It only fired a couple of rounds and stopped. We didn't know the reason then, but we knew later. Cruxy was a spy for the British. He left the column after Coolavokig, in fact he left the shagging Lewis gun behind, saying it was no good."[37]

Other witnesses reported that a man was out of position when the ambush began—Mick O'Sullivan even specified that the offender was "one of the Cork city men"—but Donovan is the only one to identify him as O'Connor. Of course, Donovan had need of a scapegoat if he and O'Hegarty had tipped off the British about the location. In essence, the IRA commanders gave away the crucial element of surprise in order to ensure a battle.

Given the confusion over the battle and O'Connor's role in it, it's fortunate that we have an unvarnished description of what happened that day from Stan Barry, the man who commanded his section and was near Cruxy throughout the ambush:

On the fourth or fifth day we were in Coolavokig, we had fifty-six rifles and twenty shotguns and two Lewis guns. I was with Conners. "Mother of Jesus" I heard one of the Auxiliaries say. "They have a quick-firing F here," for we were about twenty-five yards away from them. . . . Bill O'Brien from the city bolted. We had eight or nine men and a Lewis. . . . O'Brien jumped up with a rifle in his hand and ran and I was going to shoot him, but I didn't know that the British had seen him. The British pulled up at once and began to get out and we held our fire until someone further down fired a shot and a few of them got up the side of the hill. They were making for cover. They were only twenty-five yards away and I fired at a man four times and missed him and a man with me fired thirty-two rounds. . . . The gun jammed after five or six rounds, one burst, a jewelers job, and I gave it to Conners. Before that it was he who fired it and he carried it out of action.[38]

Thus, according to Barry, "Bás gan sagart" did actually jam, which isn't surprising, given the reports that its missing bolts had been jury-rigged and that it stopped firing after being dropped against the rocks. And Mick O'Sullivan said that after Dick Kingston carried the machine gun away, "I got it working," which suggests that it wasn't.[39]

Also, according to Barry, O'Connor didn't "give the game away" with a premature burst—they all held their fire until someone further down triggered the opening shot for the IRA. Even then they only started shooting as the Auxiliaries were climbing the hill toward them.

It appears that Cruxy was among the men sent back to the city by O'Hegarty. We know he did return, and it had to be a bitter homecoming. He had left just weeks before, dreaming of martial glory, if the stories are to be believed. Since then he'd been mocked unmercifully with "Cruxy." He'd been suspected of spying for the British because he kept a diary and asked questions. Sandow Donovan and others had scapegoated him for giving the ambush away, when it was Sandow who gave it away, by design. He'd been blamed and damned and denounced when a jury-rigged machine gun jammed after being dropped.

And O'Connor may have gotten more than just a tongue-lashing from his comrades. According to one account, "He returned to the city a few days after Coolavokig, with the story that he had been badly beaten up by the military and had a black eye to prove it."[40] Left unsaid: Exactly which military gave him the beating.

Right around this time, O'Connor was involved in a curious incident that did nothing to increase his reputation within the IRA. He told battalion headquarters that a man living on the Lee Road was planning to join the constabulary. With Danny Healy and several others, O'Connor raided the man's home, but no evidence was found to back up the accusation, so no action was taken against the man, who never did join the RIC.[41]

Once again, it seemed, Cruxy had fouled up. But that was nothing compared to the next mistake he made—carrying a gun to church.

Taking a loaded pistol to Sunday Mass was ill-advised, in more ways than one, and O'Connor should have known it. Another IRA man, Humphrey Barry, had gone to Mass that winter at St. Vincent's, none too far from Clogheen, and when the collection came his way he reached into his pocket for a few pence. What tumbled out instead was his gun. It fell to the floor and went off, winging the poor man holding the collection basket. The constabulary barracks was just fifty yards away.[42]

P. J. Murphy, a rebel officer who was with Barry during that misadventure, found himself in more trouble when he headed to Mass with a young woman on Sunday, March 20. Crown forces had thrown a cordon around the church and were conducting searches. "As we approached Clogheen chapel we were suddenly held up by a party of Black and Tans and RIC." he said. "As one of the Tans started to search me, a Constable Kelly of the RIC intervened and said he knew me and let me pass, luckily."

Down the road a piece, a comrade was less lucky: "Another party of Black and Tans had captured Paddy Connors with a revolver in his possession."[43]

O'Connor was with his brother, who managed to run away. Cruxy neither escaped nor stood his ground. For the second time in a month, he faced the British with a gun, and didn't use it—even though as a civilian caught in arms, he faced the death penalty under martial law. The first such execution had taken place just the previous month, when Con Murphy, an IRA man from North Cork, went before a firing squad at Victoria Barracks after he was captured with a revolver and ammunition.

Once in custody, O'Connor faced the same fate as Murphy if he couldn't talk his way out of it. He didn't have to think about it for very long. I'm a secret agent for the British Army, he told the police. Thus began a lengthy interrogation. After two days, he gave the police the names of "three known murderers" and the location of a safe house in Ballycannon, outside Cork.[44]

He didn't give it all away at once. And he may have thought that the names he gave would not be at the location he offered up. He didn't necessarily know that his old neighbor, Willie Deasy, and five other members of C Company would be there. They were in Blarney on the day O'Connor was captured.

He also may have assumed that if crown forces raided the Ballycannon safe house, it would either be empty, or events would go pretty much the way they had in the raid on the Bowles house in January. There, a nighttime sentry had been posted. There, everyone had gotten away except young Mary Bowles.

But no one would get away at Ballycannon. Not a single living soul.

Chapter 7

Bloodbath at Ballycannon

IT WASN'T JUST the word of Cruxy O'Connor that doomed the six boys from C Company. It was the shooting of a neighbor as a suspected informer that brought them to the Ballycannon safe house.

The IRA had been after Long Con Sheehan for months. An attendant at the mental asylum near Mount Desert, he was spotted on the way home from work talking with a plainclothes member of the RIC who was thought to be involved in intelligence work, Constable John Carroll. Maybe Sheehan's asylum uniform made him look like a constable. Or maybe the two were just passing the time of day.

Whether the conversation on January 8, 1921, was innocent or not, it struck a nerve. The sprawling asylum where Sheehan worked was a republican bastion, serving as a favored haven for IRA men on the run and as a prison for those they captured. When Dan Crowley and some other rebels saw Sheehan talking to a copper, they didn't bother to ask questions.[1]

"Hands up," yelled the gunmen.[2] Then the bullets started to fly. One hit Sheehan in the shoulder. Another clipped the constable in the wrist, wounding him slightly. Sheehan was awarded £125 in compensation.[3]

The police concluded that Sheehan had a bull's-eye on him because the IRA thought he was giving information to his friend, Constable Carroll, about rebel activity around the asylum.[4] He was thought, incorrectly, to be the informer behind the January 13 raid that almost netted O'Connor and other IRA men at the Bowles farm, which was close to the asylum's farm.

On the evening of March 19, the gunmen came calling again. Sheehan was home with his family at 198 Blarney Street when they heard a hammering on the front door. Four men were demanding to see Long Con. When his wife refused to open up, a pistol was thrust through a gap in the door and a single shot was fired. Sheehan bolted out the back, only to be stopped dead by a fusillade from an IRA squad waiting there. He went down with nine bullet wounds, as one of his sons watched helplessly.[5]

Whether Cornelius Sheehan was, in fact, an informer is debatable. It's entirely possible that he was set up by his landlady, a neighbor with whom he had been feuding. She described the recently condemned Sheehan residence as "not fit for a dog" and wanted him out. According to Sheehan's widow, the landlady, Abina Walsh, declared "I will get him another bullet."[6] And the men who gunned down Sheehan escaped over a wall to her home, which they transited to make their escape to the street.

Maybe Sheehan, unable to work since the January shooting, needed the money informing could provide—though the £125 in compensation he received would seem to suggest otherwise. It seems more plausible that, as the Sheehan family has long claimed, he was set up by his landlady, who used the IRA as a cat's-paw, ridding herself of a troublesome tenant by claiming he was an informer. The landlady certainly would not have been the first person to use the chaos of a revolution or civil war to settle a personal score—malicious denunciations come up regularly in these kinds of messy, irregular conflicts.

Long Con's killing was carried out by members of D Company, though Sheehan's home was on the turf of C Company, which presumably might have been more familiar with what was going on between Sheehan and his landlady. When they heard about the killing, six members of C Company who were hiding out near Blarney decided to head home to find out more.

"On the Sunday morning before they were done to death they had breakfast at our house," recalled Felix O'Doherty, an IRA man from Blarney. "The night before, a man named Sheehan and a suspected spy had been shot up their way. They said they were going back to Clogheen for a look around."[7]

"We tried to persuade them not to go," O'Doherty said, but the men were not to be dissuaded. "All our family pleaded with them, but it was useless. Their answer was that they would go for a look around and promised to come back that evening and to stay in our area for a time. That was the last we saw of the poor fellows."

Off they went, to their doom.

The Boys of Ballycannon

The oldest was Danny Murphy, 24, of Orrery Hill off Blarney Street. He came from a prosperous clan of pig merchants with republican sympathies—they contributed to the Tomas MacCurtain Memorial Fund in April 1920.[8] Danny had a minor brush with the law in 1915—like Michael O'Connor he was a devotee of road bowling, and it cost him a fine of two shillings.[9] Several years later he landed in more serious trouble after he and several other Volunteers beat up three British soldiers who'd been robbing shops along Blarney Street. Scooped up in a raid afterward, he spent three months in detention.[10]

Jeremiah Mullane Jr. was 22. It seems he was one of four men who helped Dan Healy try to grab a suspected spy in a Blarney Street pub in late 1920. "When we entered, he saw us and made his escape out the back of the premises," Healy recalled. "We fired a few revolver shots at him but failed to hit him."[11] Mullane was one of seven living children of a laborer from 237 Blarney Street. He was active in the Volunteers as early as 1914, according to his family. His republican ardor earned him repeated prison stints in Cork and Dublin, and he gained release with a hunger strike.[12] When he wasn't in jail, Mullane worked as a clerk in a city bakery.

Dan Crowley, twenty-two, of 171 Blarney Street, was a plasterer who had also worked at the Ford plant. He helped with Sean Moylan's escape from the mental asylum and served as an armed guard for Lord Mayor MacSwiney.[13] He was one of the members of C Company who was up in arms on Easter 1916.[14]

Tom Dennehy, twenty-one, of 164 Blarney Street, was one of seven children of Kate Dennehy, a widow. Dennehy was working as an insurance agent before he went on the run. At one point his commanding officer was his brother, Jeremiah. Dennehy was with Danny Healy and several others from C Company in April 1920 for an operation to snatch a motorized bicycle from a British soldier at Dillons Cross, about two hundred yards from Victoria Barracks. The soldier saw what was coming and tried to speed past, but Healy grabbed the handlebars, and some others grabbed the bike. Then they all high-tailed it out of there—a second bicyclist had seen what was going on, and a truckful of Tommies was barreling out of the barracks.[15]

Mick O'Sullivan, of 281 Blarney Street, had been a Volunteer since 1917. He'd been arrested three times, and gone on hunger strike—a move that so weakened him that the authorities ordered his release.[16] Before he went on the run, he'd worked as a laborer on the docks, a carpenter's apprentice, and a plumber's helper, contributing money that helped his father, a clerk, support his five siblings. At nineteen, he was the youngest of the men at Ballycannon.

The last was Willie Deasy, the O'Connors' neighbor, just twenty years old.

The addresses show that most of the six lived near Con Sheehan of 198 Blarney Street. Felix O'Doherty's account strongly suggests that the six wanted to find out more about the Sheehan killing. And so they came to Ballycannon. They arrived at Con O'Keeffe's farm on Kerry Pike late on the evening of Tuesday, March 22. They were assured of a welcome—O'Keeffe belonged to their unit, C Company.

The Raid

The evening was normal enough for Con O'Keeffe, until shortly before midnight. "About 11:30 on that night there was a knock at my door after we had all gone to bed," O'Keeffe said. "I asked, 'Who is there?' and a voice replied, 'There are a couple of us going to sleep down in the stables; give us a call at 7 in morning.'" O'Keeffe said, "all right" and went back to bed.[17] The men outside bedded down in the stables—we'll never know for sure if they posted a sentry. Perhaps they were lulled by the area's reputation as a haven for the IRA.

"Since September 1920, we had established a kind of company armed camp in the Clogheen district," Dan Healy recalled. "Here men 'on the run' slept at night in haysheds."[18]

But Holy Week, 1921, in County Cork was the wrong time and the wrong place to be lulled, if that's what happened. Just the day before, at Headford Junction in neighboring County Kerry, the rebels ambushed a train full of British soldiers; nine members of the 1st Royal Fusiliers were killed.

The crown forces had their blood up.

At 4 a.m. O'Keeffe was awakened by a thunderous knocking at the door—it was the constabulary, bellowing to be let in. They included old-line constables and newly minted Black and Tans. O'Keeffe's fumbling effort to light a lantern and open the door only enraged the policemen. The house was searched, and O'Keeffe was pulled outside to be questioned.[19] O'Keeffe later reported that he saw O'Connor on the scene. Other accounts also placed Cruxy at Ballycannon that night.[20]

While O'Keeffe was being questioned, the police found the six men in the stable. "As they were speaking to me, I heard one of the boys roaring as if he was being tortured," O'Keeffe said. "I then saw one of the boys being pushed across a field."

"He is showing where the arms are," said a Black and Tan. The prisoner was brought back to the stable, and the shooting began. "I heard a shot," O'Keeffe said. "Then at intervals there were two or three shots, and then a volley of shots." When he complained that all the shooting would make his family in the house "go mad," an officer responded, "What did the people do the other day when they fired into the train at Headford Junction?"

Word spread that some of the prisoners had escaped, and then there were "some terrible volleys fired from where the boys were," O'Keeffe recalled.

It seems clear that the "escape" was a pretext—that the police had captured the rebels, told them to run, then shot them as they fled. Jeremiah O'Flaherty, who lived across Kerry Pike from the O'Keeffe farm, was awakened by gunshots around 4:30 a.m. and looked out the window. "I heard a man screaming, and I heard another voice saying, 'Run for it.'" he said. "He ran for about 20 yards and then a volley of shots fired. Volleys came about every ten minutes after that."[21]

It was by no means unusual for the authorities to order captured IRA men to run, so they could shoot them for trying to escape.[22] Jeremiah's brother, Morgan, recalled several volleys between 4:30 and 5:30 a.m. The police brought the bodies out in blankets. Six lorries arrived at 6:30 a.m. to collect the dead. "As the lorries were coming, the police on the road who had been at O'Keeffe's farm started cheering," Morgan O'Flaherty said.[23]

Thus dawned Holy Wednesday, or "Spy Wednesday" as it was known in Ireland, because it was the day Judas betrayed Jesus.

O'Connor's betrayal made for a bloody night's work—and a senseless waste. Had the six men been interrogated, one or more might have broken, and revealed more hiding places, like the O'Doherty home in Blarney. But revenge trumped reason, as it often does in civil wars, and so the six surrendered their young lives to a vengeful constabulary that wanted to send a message, written in blood.

The authorities told the world the six had been killed in a gunfight during a raid: "The occupants of the shed, becoming aware of the cordon drawn around them, opened fire with revolvers, and both sides became hotly engaged. A number of individual combats took place, and all six were killed."[24] But the government had trouble keeping its story straight—a court of inquiry held in lieu of an inquest found that the six were killed trying to escape. Few in Cork fell for either story; the killings quickly became a byword for mindless official brutality. As Felix O'Doherty put it, "the massacre of the poor lads by Tans at Ballycannon shocked every decent-minded person."

We'll never know the full story of exactly what happened, because everyone on one side died there that night, and everyone on the other side had a motive to cover up the nature of the massacre. But as at Coolavokig, Stan Barry of C Company was in a good position to shed some light on the events at Ballycannon. He was quite nearly the seventh man to die there.

Barry had spent the night before with the men, staying at a different farm. They decided to "chance sleeping without a lookout, so they dumped all their stuff"—two bombs and four revolvers—because they wouldn't have had a chance if they were surrounded. "We slept in an open shed, awoke around 10 a.m. on straw."[25]

They walked to Clogheen the next day, but lorries full of Auxiliaries were buzzing around, so they left. "I arranged to meet the six at 10:30 at Conny Keeffe's in Ballycannon and I went to meet a girl, and I left at 12 and I had never slept in this place, so I couldn't find them. I went back across a field into a hayshed."

"I am assuming now that the night they were murdered they dumped their stuff again," he said, speculating that "they couldn't stand the rigorous sentry duty at night."[26] After moving elsewhere and bedding down for the night, Barry never heard a thing. It was a shock to everyone when he showed up alive afterward. "The next day I appeared as a ghost, for everyone was certain I had been massacred with the others."[27]

The condition of the bodies, each shot multiple times, gave rise to false rumors of torture and mutilation. An account of the scene in the *Cork Examiner* described pools of blood at O'Keeffe's farm, and a piece of a tongue stuck to a fencepost.[28] Michael Collins's biographer, Piaras Beaslai, elaborated with grotesque, and erroneous details: "They cut out the tongue of one, the nose of another, the heart of another, and battered in the skull of the fourth."[29]

Willy Deasy's brother, Jeremiah, got stuck with the horrifying task of helping to identify the bodies. An eighteen-year-old clerk (and member of C Company), he showed up at the mortuary shed of Victoria Barracks on Thursday, March 24. He'd known all six of the dead men. He accompanied the bodies to Cork's Catholic Cathedral, where they were examined by doctors and prepared for burial. The postmortem examinations supported the idea that the six had been gunned down after they were captured and refuted the notion of torture and mutilation.

"It was obvious that the young men had been told to run, when revolver and rifle or machine-gun bullets were fired point blank at them," wrote Seamus Fitzgerald, a republican publicist who attended the postmortem. "The majority of the entrance wounds were in the rear, but some of the bullets caught the men as they were falling, causing terrible wounds."[30]

"Some of these wounds were of such a nature as to give rise to the rumor that they had been mutilated after death, and I had to correct such an insinuation."

If republican activists seemed obsessed with the gory details of the deaths, well, what good was a tale of martyrdom that didn't emphasize the agonies endured for the faith? The six deaths also spoke to the city's lingering shame about not joining in the blood sacrifice that was Easter 1916. When Dublin rose, Cork balked, and local republicans had felt guilty about it ever since. Now, in some small way, Cork had made amends. The six dead joined the republican pantheon of executed prisoners, with Pearse and Connolly.

And there would be a great, grand funeral, just in time for the fifth anniversary of Easter 1916.

The British grasped what was going on and limited the funeral to 150 people. They put armored cars and lorries full of troops at the head of the cortege. They banned republican flags. They thought they could somehow dam a sea of tears, but the British soon learned they were battling an invulnerable tide of grief. The city had lost six of its sons.

Mourners massed along the three-mile route from the cathedral to the cemetery to pay their quiet respects: "A dense crowd of people filled Patrick Street, and as the procession filed slowly along in the brilliant sunshine, no sound was heard but the dull tread of those marching, the solemn tolling of the church bells and the burring noise of the heavy lorries." Fifty priests attended the graveside services as the six were laid to rest in the republican plot in St. Finbarr's Cemetery.[31]

Once the elaborate ceremony was complete, the Cork IRA turned its attention toward finding the man responsible for the mass funeral. What Cruxy didn't realize when he talked to the police was that some members of the police were talking to the Irish Republican Army. Specifically, they were talking to Pa Murray's sister, Eily.

Eily had two sources in the Royal Irish Constabulary—Sergeant Flanagan and Constable O'Brien.[32] Flanagan was a neighbor and friend of the family, the kind of guy who could be counted on to tip off the boys when an arrest or police raid was planned. Constable O'Brien was a different matter. He made contact only after the Ballycannon killings, apparently outraged by the slaughter, and his words were pure gold. First, he warned Eily that the police were after her brother. And then he told her who had led the police to O'Keeffe's barn in Ballycannon.

"There was an IRA man arrested about that time, and it was he who took out those policemen. Six were killed that night," she said. "O'Brien told me it was this fellow who got those men murdered. O'Connor was his name."

The news that O'Connor was an informer set off a scramble in the IRA—in addition to knowing the safe houses, he knew the location of the arms depots where the secret army had stashed its weapons. The machinery had to be moved, and quickly.

They got some of the stuff out, because Cruxy didn't give away the locations right away—he talked about them only in a subsequent interrogation. So men started showing up in houses across Cork with passels of pistols to be carefully wrapped and hidden under piles of coal. But they didn't get it all. Armed with O'Connor's information, crown forces raided two depots, and came away with "two motorcars and a motorcycle, a quantity of rifles, revolvers, bombs, ammunition of various calibers and a large quantity of stolen Government property."[33]

Once they'd salvaged as much ordnance as possible, O'Connor's ex-comrades had a chance to absorb the full enormity of what he had done. Traitors and informers like Cruxy were insiders, and thus considered by the IRA to be a far more dangerous threat than a mere spy sent in from the outside.

And Cruxy wasn't some civilian passing along pub gossip—he was one of their own. He knew where the bodies—and the guns—were buried. He hadn't just betrayed a cause, or some comrades in arms he'd only recently met. He'd given up men he had known since childhood and turned his back on the community that nurtured him. It was all very personal, in a way that only a revolution and a civil war can be.

And so it was time to arrange a funeral for another member of C Company. He wasn't dead yet—in fact, he was holed up in the most secure British facility in Cork. But there were ways. Matters could be arranged. Cruxy O'Connor would be sorted out.

With a healthy dose of strychnine.

Chapter 8

A Basketful of Poison

IT WAS HIS mother who saved O'Connor from eating the poisoned dinner—and then only by the skin of her teeth.

Sandow Donovan, by now the commander of the Cork IRA's elite Active Service Unit, had held a grudge against O'Connor ever since the machine-gun incident at the Coolavokig ambush, which Donovan had led. The butchery at Ballycannon only made him more bound and determined that Connors the spy desperately needed to die.

"Dan Donovan—he wanted this man poisoned in jail. They wanted this man poisoned and I had to take on the job," said Nora Martin, local commander of Cumann na mBan, a sort of women's auxiliary of the IRA.[1] So Martin had a meal made up with enough strychnine to "poison a regiment."

Cooking it was the easy part. The tough part was who would take on the risky job of delivering it to Victoria Barracks, where O'Connor was being held. "It was a hot time, frightfully dangerous, and I looked around Cork and all the members and outside the members and eventually I hit on Mrs. Cuthbert," Martin said.

At the time, Mrs. Cuthbert was Ethel Condon, a dedicated Cumann member who came from a family of rebels—she had two brothers and a boyfriend in the IRA. A trained machinist, she graduated from putting up subversive posters to making bombs and bullets in the back of Andy Ahern's boot shop on Grattan Street.[2]

That bit of moonlighting came to a shattering end when the makeshift munitions factory blew up in May 1918. The blast killed one Volunteer,

73

Michael Tobin, and injured several others, including Condon's boyfriend, Sean O'Connell, who "was blown clean through a window."[3]

Fortunately for Ethel Condon, she wasn't on the premises at the time. And fortunately for the republican movement, she wasn't deterred from the kind of risky, covert assignments that were becoming essential in the intelligence war raging in the streets of Cork. In the fall of 1920, she and a friend, Nellie O'Connell, were asked to use their charms to lure a couple of Black and Tans into a trap, so the IRA could seize some ciphers they were carrying.

"I had to go and try to meet Tans," she said. "There were two particular men who always stood under Mangan's clock in [St.] Patrick Street, and our men were always anxious to get documents they had on them."[4]

"I paraded up and down Patrick Street just to draw their attention to me."

The Tans fell for the bait. Condon and O'Connell led them to a quiet spot by the asylum for the blind near city hall. The women had to keep smiles on their faces and a gleam in their eyes, chatting and charming, all the while fearing that bullets might fly at any moment. "Having to act as decoy for the IRA to capture two Black and Tans placed me between two fires if they should have discovered the ruse and used firearms," Condon said.[5] Again, her luck held out. The IRA showed up, and the girls, feigning surprise and fright, ran away as the victims were relieved of the documents.

Condon's skills as an actress were growing. They were put to the test in April 1921 with the killing of a suspected spy, Denis "Din Din" Donovan. Condon knew Din Din well—he had worked with her at the munitions factory, and together they had transported smuggled guns brought in by boat. Now she was lugging the rifle to be used in his killing. It was a two-mile trek through the city, from Nora Martin's house at Warren Place to the Wellington Bridge (now the Thomas Davis Bridge). She hid it under her long coat, gripping the loop through the pocket, the barrel pointed up.

Martin, who'd given her the gun, described the kind of nerves needed for the job: "Dodging through lanes and alleys with the gun that you know is intended to be used for the killing of an enemy, never thinking of your own danger, but hoping to get there in time and that the operation will be successful." Condon got there in time. The operation was successful. Din Din was killed. But then came the hard part—a bit of acting that would unnerve even a professional. The job: Spy on Din Din's wake.

Richard Murphy, an IRA captain, wanted to know if the victim's family was going to finger anyone in the killing. He had a very personal interest in the answer. "He asked me one evening coming from work—coming from town—would I do him a favor and I said I would if it was in my power, and he asked me—there was a spy being shot and he said 'You know him well, Din Din.'" Murphy wanted her to go to the wake, and listen to what the family had to say about the death.[6]

So off she went: "I went in and knelt down and said a prayer like any ordinary person." And she was all ears when Din Din's father spoke. "He said he knew there used to be two of them coming there every night before he was murdered looking for him and he mentioned two names, Richard Murphy and Cornie McCarthy. I came back and reported that to Richard Murphy."

The same Richard Murphy who had assigned her the mission. And who, forewarned, managed to avoid capture.

But Ethel's greatest performance was her role as Paddy O'Connor's mother. She didn't mind taking on the assignment; she knew about the butchery at Ballycannon. She'd had to stash some guns hurriedly removed from an arms depot in Clogheen after Cruxy talked.

But that was just a warm-up act—the big show was the poison scheme. And for that, she needed a lot of nerve—"It was a very grave risk"—and an appropriate costume, because she wouldn't be playing a temptress or a mourner. "I was disguised in old shoes and a shawl, dressed just like his mother would have been," she said.[7] They'd been spying on Mrs. O'Connor and had found a basket that looked like the one she used to bring her son food at the detention barracks. Condon was to deliver the basket of food and wait until the basket was returned to her, so she could prove to rebel commanders that the delivery had been made.

Everything was in place, but for the poison plot to work, some IRA men had to detain the real Mrs. O'Connor far from the barracks.

They failed spectacularly.

Mrs. O'Connor had already lost two sons—she was not about to lose a third. When it came to a squad of gunmen vs. a plucky, protective sixty-two-year-old mother, the odds were clear: The gunmen never had a chance. "Apparently they had her in a very public place where she lived and she began to yell and roar, with the result that they let her loose," Nora Martin said. "She must have suspected something—she made for the jail."[8]

And there the real Mrs. O'Connor nearly bumped into the fake Mrs. O'Connor. It happened when Condon got the basket back, after what must have seemed an interminable wait. As she exited the place, there was Cruxy's mother, marching up the other side of the walk.

"I had only got outside the barrack gate when I saw Mrs. O'Connor going in," Condon recalled. "If she had arrived a few minutes sooner, it would have almost certainly cost me my life, as the moment she arrived inside with her basket, the previous one was detected."[9] As the alarm rose, she slipped away, lest her brief visit to the detention barracks become a permanent one.

And Paddy O'Connor lived to eat another day, thanks to a very gutsy mother who buried two too many sons. But a man's strengths can be his weaknesses. When, shortly after the poisoning attempt, the British moved O'Connor out of Cork, it was Cruxy's ongoing links to his family that left a trail of breadcrumbs for the Irish Republican Army to follow.

At first, the British planned to transfer him to Dublin by train, via Blarney Station, according to one account. The story has it that a party of twelve gunmen showed up at the station to escort him on a much longer trip—into the next world—so that plan had to be scrapped.[10]

Instead, O'Connor was smuggled out of Cork on a Royal Navy destroyer, dressed like a seaman, and showed up in London with £150 in his pocket and a couple of police detectives on his coattails as bodyguards.

With Cruxy out of reach, the IRA turned its attention to the British spymaster, Captain Kelly. The job fell to an elite squad formed around the time of the Coolavokig ambush.[11] Commanded by Sean Twomey, the active service unit included Pa Murray and Danny Healy, and it devoted a lot of its time to the messy work of eliminating suspected informers and intelligence threats.

So diligent were the unit's efforts that all the bloodletting drove its commander over the edge. "This particular type of work was very severe on Twomey," Murray recalled. "It was beginning to affect his nerves."

It came to a head one Saturday morning as Murray and Twomey were staking out the Cork jail, where Kelly was due to arrive. "Twomey became mentally affected, and he asked me to take him out and shoot him," Murray said. While Murray took Twomey home, their quarry escaped: "During this time, Kelly had gone up to the jail in an open car and returned from it in an armored car."[12]

On the morning of Monday, May 23, the unit had another go at Kelly.

Two groups from the unit and an intelligence officer, Michael Kenny, took positions along Washington Street in the center of Cork—the plan was for Kenny to signal Murray when Kelly passed by in a car. If Murray didn't get him, the second group would. Kenny had played the same role in the attempt to kidnap General Strickland, when Kelly was sitting next to the general in the car—and the result was pretty much the same. The man from Knock pulled off another miracle.

"Captain Kelly came from the jail in an open car on this particular morning and had practically passed the intelligence officer before he was recognized," Murray said. "When we got the signal, the car had passed us, and we signaled to the men further down."[13]

"The car was going so fast that it was practically past them before they threw the bombs. One bomb was thrown into the car but failed to explode. The second bomb hit the hood of the car and rolled on to the roadway. Some shots were also exchanged, but Kelly escaped."

Kelly had a knack for surviving the best-laid ambushes. He'd survived the Strickland attack. He avoided the honey trap that Pa Murray and Danny Healy had set for him in December 1920. Then there was the time an IRA squad lay in wait for him after a dance at Victoria Barracks, only to be thwarted by the unexpected appearance of a large British Army patrol.[14] Kelly had also ducked the Dillons Cross ambush that led to the burning of central Cork. The man seemed to have nineteen lives, so it was time for the IRA to try its luck elsewhere.

Cruxy had been located in London, thanks to a letter he sent his family, and a sighting by an old acquaintance.

Given the number of Irish in London, it wasn't long before somebody O'Connor knew from Cork ran into him on the street, guarded by a couple of detectives. The sister of Sean Murray, who served with him in the flying column, spotted O'Connor, and damned if the two didn't strike up a sidewalk conversation, like the old acquaintances that they were.

"She saw him in London where she lived, with two strange men beside him, and her husband said 'they're 'tecs,'" Murray recalled. "She spoke to Connors, asking him how I was, and he chatted away with her."[15] Then the detectives joined the conversation, with a little gallows humor about the gunmen they knew were stalking O'Connor. "These two fellows are after Connors, and they might shoot us by mistake," one told Murray's brother-in-law.

The two fellows after O'Connor were named Danny Healy and Liam O'Callaghan.

Healy got the Cruxy job the day after a truce with Britain was signed in July 1921—there would be no cease-fire in the IRA's pursuit of the informer. As Healy relaxed in a cafe owned by the wife of Sean O'Hegarty, he got the word that O'Connor was in London, and was expected to collect a letter from his family on a certain date. It was Healy's job to find him and ensure that he never got his hands on that or any other letter.

"Liam O'Callaghan and I were to go to London and shoot Connors when he arrived at Hammersmith Post Office," he said.[16]

The next day they left by train for Dublin, where Michael Collins gave them a note for the IRA intelligence chief in London, Sam Maguire, a noted

Gaelic football player—the Sam Maguire Cup given annually to the winners of Ireland's Gaelic football championship is named for him.

Healy and O'Callaghan arrived in London on July 10, 1921, and met Maguire. Maguire, in turn, passed them on to Sean Flood, the rebel who had accidentally slammed straight into Prime Minister Lloyd George in the Westminster tube station. With Flood's aid, Healy and O'Callaghan set up a stakeout at the post office.

But it was all for naught.

"For about ten days we waited in the vicinity of Hammersmith, but failed to see Connors," Healy said. "We then decided we had missed him and we returned to Cork."

O'Connor, aware that he was being stalked, had moved on to Liverpool, a major embarkation point to America. His unshakeable bonds with his family had nearly gotten him killed once again, and not for the last time. The IRA's vast trans-Atlantic network of friends and sympathizers was watching and listening for any sign of him. Sooner or later, Cruxy was bound to be spotted.

The job of tracking O'Connor fell to one of the most unlikely couples to come out of the Irish revolution. He was a fresh-faced draper's assistant who rose to become the top rebel intelligence officer in Cork. She was a dark, haunted beauty, a policeman's daughter and soldier's widow who worked as the chief clerk at British headquarters in Cork.

They fell in love when he kidnapped her child.

Chapter 9

The Spying Game

SHE PROVED AS adept at stealing secrets as she was at keeping them. The secrets she stole got men killed; the secrets she kept embraced love and marriage. Jo Marchment worked simultaneously for two archrival intelligence chiefs, but if there was a true spymaster among the trio, she was the one who always seemed to get her way—and get away with it.

She was born Mary Josephine McCoy on September 10, 1891, in Adare, County Limerick, the youngest of Henry and Bridget McCoy's six surviving children.[1] Just nine months before, her father had been appointed the head constable in Adare. About twelve years later, he retired from the Royal Irish Constabulary, and the family moved to Cork city. His daughter went by her middle name, often shortened to Jo.

After a typical middle-class Catholic childhood—Saints Peter and Paul National School and St. Aloysius School—she took a course in secretarial skills, shorthand, and typing. Her plans for a career were interrupted when her sister, who had married an Englishman in Wales, became pregnant with a second child. Jo went over to help. There she caught the eye of a traveling salesman, Coleridge Marchment, and when she moved to Newport, Wales, to work as a governess, Marchment visited, and informed her he was converting to Roman Catholicism. (Such a shift was not out of character—after a bankruptcy he had changed his last name from Brown to Marchment.)

A romance ensued, followed by marriage, but there was a big caveat. Though they were married in Wales, where Marchment's parents lived in

Cadoxton, "He did not tell his parents of the marriage at the time, and I did not tell mine," she recalled.[2]

Perhaps it was because her in-laws, the Browns, were staunch Protestants, and would not have been thrilled with their son's conversion to Roman Catholicism. Even after their son Reggie was born on November 23, 1913, neither could bring themselves to tell their parents the news. Her mother died in March 1914 without ever knowing of either the marriage or the grandchild.

World War I spoiled the carefully guarded secret.

"Some time after the outbreak of the war in August 1914, my husband was called up for army service and he then decided to acquaint his parents with our marriage," she recalled. "We were invited to live with them for the duration of the war." It was far from an ideal arrangement: "Living with my husband's parents and their two daughters was a constant strain. They were hostile to Catholics and did not wish a Catholic in the house."

In addition to the sectarian issues, there were others: "I had many difficulties and hardships. My husband's eldest sister Maud was a teacher, a very dominating character who took control of the whole household." A younger Brown sister, meanwhile, appointed herself as Reggie's nanny, "and gradually I felt my little son was taken over entirely by her."

Another secret intruded.

"I was informed that my husband had two letters, one to me and one to his parents, which were to be opened in the event of his death," she said. The letters were written after one of Marchment's sisters had visited him, but his wife was never told what the two discussed. The mounting strains took a toll, and when Jo had a second child, Gerald, in August 1916, it became unbearable. She resolved to decamp to Ireland. "When I told my people-in-law I was going back to Cork the grandparents were very upset and begged me to leave Reggie with them for a while," she said. "After a lot of persuasion, and most unwillingly I unfortunately agreed to this."

Barely two months later, in October, Henry McCoy died in Cork. Her husband was in the army, her young son was in Wales, and now her father was in the grave. Josephine went to work at the Ministry of Pensions office—she had Gerald to raise, and the Browns were demanding more money for Reggie's upkeep. When her boss retired, she took a better job at British Army headquarters in Victoria Barracks.

The whole time, the contents of those two letters nagged at her: "It was hoped that he would come back and destroy both letters."[3] But he never came back.

In the summer of 1917 came the battle of Passchendaele, which Lloyd George called one of the greatest disasters of the war (itself one of the greatest catastrophes of the century). After years of bloody stalemate on the Western Front, the British high command settled on a summer offensive against the Germans in Flanders. Battle was joined on July 31, and after three months of some of the worst fighting in all the war, the British Army had little to show for it, despite horrific casualties.

If insanity is doing the same thing over and over again and expecting different results, the British high command was certifiably mad. It tried again.

On October 30, Private Coleridge Marchment of the Yorkshire Regiment's 3rd Battalion clambered over the lip of the trenches with his comrades and marched into what amounted to "fifty square miles of slime and filth from which every shell that burst threw up ghastly relics, and raised stenches too abominable to describe; and over all, and dominating all, a never-ceasing ear-shattering artillery fire."[4]

Private Marchment died in that hell.

He left behind two young sons and a widow, whose own fight was just beginning. The secret letters that her husband had written in case of his death now came back to haunt Josephine—they stipulated that he wanted his children raised as Protestants. She had to go to court for custody of Reggie and in the summer of 1918, a judge in London ruled against her. She lacked the money for an appeal, and in any case legal advisers told her in November—the month the war ended—that there was no hope of winning. Britain had stolen her first-born child.

"Every legal avenue appeared to be closed," she recalled.[5]

Of course, in postwar Cork, there were other, not-so-legal, avenues for redress. After a period of profound depression—Jo said she considered drowning herself in the River Lee—she made preliminary contact with the Irish Republican Army while spending time in the town of Youghal in 1919. The contact, the adjutant of the local IRA unit, Mike Walsh, used her for some small jobs—passing messages and contacting some prisoners. Perhaps he did not fully trust the widow of a British soldier and daughter of a police sergeant. Or perhaps he was testing her. Either way, things heated up in September after she returned to Cork city.

As Jo tells it, she was upset at another demand from the Browns for money for Reggie's care, and went to Holy Trinity Church, seeking solace at an altar devoted to the Virgin Mary. A kindly old Capuchin brother noticed her tears and suggested she talk to one of the priests, and thus she came face-to-face with Father Dominic O'Connor. He just happened to be the

IRA chaplain for Cork city, and the brother of Joe O'Connor, the quarter-master of the Cork brigade.

"I poured out my troubles to Father Dominic," she said. "He was most sympathetic and helpful, and at the end of our conversation said with reassuring confidence, 'I will get your child back for you.'"[6]

That a woman seeking to spy for the IRA would by chance bumble into the IRA's chaplain in a city the size of Cork can be explained only as the work of divine providence (as Jo suggested), as an extraordinary coincidence, or, just possibly, as a carefully arranged handoff from the Youghal IRA to the leadership of the Cork city brigade after Josephine had proven her bona fides.

She later told her children that her motives were patriotic: "No one living in Cork at that time could fail to be aware to some extent of the struggle that was developing between the British authorities and the Irish people, then led by Sinn Fein and the Irish Volunteers. . . . My sympathies were then with the Volunteers and I felt I could and should help them."

But the transactional nature of what was going on seems clear. After Father Dominic made his remarkable promise to a stranger to recover her son from the legal custody of his grandparents across the sea, they discussed how she should contact the Cork city brigade. She gave him a piece of paper with the letter G on it. A few nights later a young man visited her and handed her back the slip of paper.

And thus did Jo Marchment and Florrie O'Donoghue become a part of each other's lives, and their nation's history, in the wilderness of mirrors that was revolutionary Cork.

The Florrie O'Donoghue Story

He grew up gazing at the breasts of a goddess, near a brook shimmering with ancient glory.

The breasts were the Paps of Anu, two rounded hills along the Kerry-Cork county line named for the mother of the gods in Irish mythology. Matching cairns at the summits mimic the earth mother's nipples. A stream runs between the hills; legend says that it was here that Finn McCool, the giant leader of a warrior brotherhood called the Fianna, avenged a comrade by spearing his killer on Samhain, the ancient Celtic Halloween.[7] In Ireland, ancient or modern, bloody payback always seemed to fall around holidays.

Florence O'Donoghue (Florrie to his friends) was raised on his family's farm in Rathmore, County Kerry, in the bosom of these hills: "Since early childhood I had learned to watch for the mountain stream, which, after rain, shone like a bright ribbon of silver flowing from the little lake at the base of their rounded breasts."[8]

His father had been a rebel, jailed during the Land War of the 1880s, when Ireland's long-oppressed tenant farmers stood up to the landlords who ruled their vast estates from manor houses, or their townhouses in London.

Though Florrie was an only son and stood to inherit the farm, he had no more interest in wresting a living from the land than his father had in detailing the struggle to wrest the land from the Earl of Kenmare. The old man only ever joked about the Land War—the O'Donoghues were a family that knew how to keep their mouths shut and their eyes wide open.

At age sixteen, a wide-eyed Florrie left his parents and five sisters for a new life as a draper's apprentice with his cousin in Cork city.

O'Donoghue was soon homesick and hid his loneliness behind books. He joined the Cork Catholic Young Men's Society for its library, bought himself a bicycle, and went to night school. When the Great War broke out in 1914, he, like a great number of Irishmen, had no interest in joining the fighting. Nor did he have any interest in joining the revolutionary politics of those who wanted an independent Ireland. In fact, the republican movement's existence barely registered with him.

All that changed, utterly, at Easter, 1916.

On Easter Sunday, an older cousin, Patrick O'Connor—no relation to Cruxy—paid a visit as Florrie labored in the draper's shop. It was a busy day, and Florrie didn't have much time for his cousin, who was in town for his brother's funeral, and had been drinking. O'Connor, a postal clerk in Dublin, morosely predicted that Florrie would never see him again, then left.

Within days, the prediction came true with the Easter Uprising. Patrick O'Connor, postal clerk and Irish Volunteer, was killed in the fighting around the General Post Office.[9] Florrie hadn't even known his cousin was mixed up in the republican movement. In fact, O'Connor was a captain in the Volunteers and a member of the Irish Republican Brotherhood. His body was never found, so Florrie never did see him again, even in death.

Just as Josephine Marchment's life was forever changed by an act of military insanity—Passchendaele—so too was Florrie's by the glorious madness of the Easter Rising.

"For me and for thousands of others, the Rising was an illumination, a lifting of the mental horizon giving glimpses of an undiscovered country," he recalled. "It created an interest more intense and absorbing than anything in my previous experience."[10]

That winter, O'Donoghue joined the Irish Volunteers. He went far, quickly, thanks in part to the bicycle he'd bought after coming to Cork. In the spring of 1917, he was entrusted with dispatches from the Cork brigade's commander, Tomas MacCurtain, then he was named the lieutenant of an IRA cyclists company, under Denis MacNeilus. When MacNeilus was arrested in 1918, O'Donoghue was promoted to captain of the cyclists company. By early 1919, he was organizing the Cork brigade's intelligence service, the job that would in just a few months bring him to Jo Marchment, and her child custody problem.[11]

Jo the Spy

O'Donoghue had known about Marchment since the summer of 1919, thanks to her Youghal contact, but his first sight of her, when he called at her home that September, was a revelation: "a young and very lovely girl. I had not expected that."[12]

This lovely woman was also a mother lode of military intelligence. By 1919, Josephine was the forewoman clerk at the headquarters of the British Army's Sixth Division in Victoria Barracks. She had access to the files of the division's commander, General Peter Strickland, including the intelligence department. She also served as confidential secretary to Strickland's chief staff officer, Captain Webb, and to his chief intelligence officer, Captain Kelly.[13] Her duties included making copies of reports, which made it easy to smuggle out an extra copy.

At first, her contact was Florrie. They discovered they had previously seen each other, if not met, when she went to the shop where he worked on Castle Street—both remembered the fleeting glimpse. Sometimes he went to her house, more often they met in churches, but she found those rendezvous "less satisfying"—a hint that perhaps their relationship was deepening. For a time, they met daily, low voices in the hush of a nave, alive to the danger yet each entrusting their life to the other.

Eventually, Florrie concluded that their meetings were too big a risk, that they were probably under surveillance, that he would have to step back if she was to remain an agent in place. "I constantly met him until it became dangerous," she said.[14] "We met at different churches, and things were beginning to get hot and we were watched and under suspicion, rather he thought we were watched, and it was decided upon that this should be discontinued."

Intermediaries stepped in.

However much she missed seeing Florrie, Josephine approached her espionage mission with cold calculation. Her first order of business was an office purge. "When I undertook to help the IRA Intelligence movement, I studied my whole situation," she said. "I looked into the personnel that were around me in the Sixth Division."[15] After hard scrutiny of any who might pose a problem for her spying, she used her influence to ensure that three were fired.

The next step: Charming her way into the good graces of the division's intelligence officers, via their children. "I would like you to stress how I got in with the Intelligence department," she told Irish officials considering her pension application years later. "I had to use my discretion in making my place secure beforehand, because on that account I was teaching the staff officers' children, and I was well in with them."[16]

With problematic colleagues dismissed and the divisional staff disarmed, Jo launched her real work. Before she was done, a flood of intelligence had flowed out of Victoria Barracks.

She provided the rebels with codes, with minutes of the Sixth Division's staff conference, with photographs or physical descriptions of British officers, with their movements and home addresses.[17] The latter came in handy when the IRA retaliated against officers considered too brutal by burning their homes in England.

When the British planted an informer among IRA prisoners, Jo got the word out.

When the British planned a major sweep through the mountains of West Cork and East Kerry, Jo smuggled out details of the planned operation.

When a civilian informer told Captain Kelly that the leadership of the Cork city brigade usually took a certain route just before curfew, Jo didn't have time to make a copy. So she smuggled the original letter out of the building and showed it to the IRA's commander in Cork, thus thwarting a British ambush. The informer didn't live to see another sunrise.

In fact, bodies were turning up all over Cork as the result of Jo's work. Years later, she laid it all out, in chilling detail: "As a result of information given by me concerning the movement of members of this Staff three British Intelligence Officers were captured by the IRA at Waterfall near Cork, in November 1920. These officers were wearing civilian clothes and were subsequently executed."

"I secured information in several cases where civilians had sent in information relating to the IRA. Six civilians were executed as a result."[18]

Remarkably, among the six civilians were two close neighbors—James and Frederick Blemens. The pair—a middle-class Protestant father and son—were abducted, then shot in December 1920 as suspected members of a supposed British spy ring connected to the Cork YMCA, after Josephine reported suspicious meetings at their home.[19]

It's quite a coincidence that a pair of spies for the crown just happened to be living practically next door to a spy for the Irish Republican Army. Mick Murphy, an IRA commander, insisted he was given their names by a youth named Parsons, who had admitted to being part of a British spy ring based in the predominantly Protestant YMCA. And Murphy said Parsons's information on Frederick and James Blemens was corroborated by other evidence: "We also had information about them from letters captured by our lads in raids on postmen for mails."[20]

So maybe Jo really did spot a pair of spies, though there are plenty of doubts that they were guilty of anything other than loyalist sentiments and living too close to a woman who was doing a lot of her own spying.

The Blemens firing squad included one "Florrie Donoghue."[21] But it wasn't Jo's Florrie—there was another Florrie O'Donoghue active in the Cork IRA. The firing squad member had to be this man, because Jo's Florrie was off in Wales at the time, kidnapping her son.

The Welsh Job

Jo was determined to get Reggie back from her Welsh in-laws. So determined, in fact, that when she grew impatient with progress on the project, she made an appointment to see Florrie's superior, Terence MacSwiney, about the matter.

The meeting in the lord mayor's city hall office was scheduled for just about the time that it was raided by Captain Kelly and a horde of British troops, in the opening act of MacSwiney's martyrdom. Jo said she was delayed by a neighbor; Florrie said she "fortunately escaped" what would have happened if she had been caught by the British meeting with MacSwiney, the head of the Cork IRA.[22]

In fact, Florrie said, he had been making progress on the Reggie project. It was just that he insisted on handling the thing personally: "When the question arose of putting the matter into the hands of our men in England, I opposed it. From the beginning I said I would go over myself if permitted."[23]

After MacSwiney's arrest, he was permitted. Michael Collins, the IRA's director of intelligence and de facto leader, gave the green light, and by

The Semple School for Girls
241 Central Park West
New York City

After Patrick "Cruxy" O'Connor was gunned down in Manhattan, onlookers lifted him onto the step of the Semple School for Girls, which was on the northwest corner of 84th Street and Central Park West.

The hillside Sunday's Well district of Cork city was home to Cruxy O'Connor and the IRA comrades who tracked him down in New York. The white building standing alone at left just below the ridge line was the Mount Desert estate near the O'Connor home.

Willie Deasy (*left*), one of six IRA men killed when O'Connor turned informer, posing with comrades in Cork. His brother Jerry (*right*) helped identify the six bodies. (Courtesy of the Deasy family)

After an IRA attack on December 11, 1920, British forces burned a swath of central Cork in retaliation, including O'Connor's workplace.

Cork residents lined the streets to pay their silent respects to the six IRA men killed at Ballycannon as the funeral procession passed on Easter Sunday, 1921. The authorities put armored cars and trucks full of troops at the head of the cortege.

Father Dominic O'Connor (*center*), the chaplain of the Cork city IRA, in London for the inquest into the death of Terence MacSwiney, the lord mayor of Cork. Father O'Connor played a key role in recruiting Josephine Marchment as an IRA spy in the British military headquarters in Cork.

O'Connor was interrogated at what was then Victoria Barracks, the center of British military power in Cork. When he turned informer, the IRA very nearly killed him there with a poisoned meal brought in by a woman disguised as his mother.

Jimmy McGee, a New York union official and waterfront fixer for the IRA, provided the guns for the O'Connor ambush. About a year earlier, he played a key role in a daring plot to smuggle 500 tommy guns to Ireland aboard a freighter docked in Hoboken, N.J.

A federal Customs official with some of the hundreds of Ireland-bound tommy guns confiscated from the *SS East Side*. The seizure led to a confrontation between Customs officials and the Hoboken police, who sympathized with the IRA. (Granger Historical Picture Archive)

November 1920 O'Donoghue was in Britain with Jack Cody, the same IRA driver who had helped Pa Murray in stalking the cabinet. Florrie's contacts there had trouble arranging a car (transportation seemed to be a perpetual problem when the boys ventured overseas). Holed up in Cardiff, appalled at the possibility of letting down Josephine and the IRA, Florrie became so desperate that they went out one night to hijack a car. His only scruple: Whatever the vehicle, it had to have but one occupant.

"By some providential good luck, we did not see that night a single car with a driver only, and we walked back to some Cardiff lodging house disappointed and miserable," he recalled.[24]

The morning brought better news—Sean Phelan, a Volunteer from Liverpool, arrived to announce that a car was on the way. Without waiting for the car to arrive, the normally calculating O'Donoghue again took another uncharacteristically rash step. He launched the kidnapping via taxi. With Cody and Phelan, he headed off by cab to the Brown home in Cadoxton.

Depending on who you believe, the kidnappers either shoved a gun in Mr. Brown's face and threatened to "blow his brains out" (the newspaper version from the *South Wales Echo*) or they "did not show any weapons" (Florrie's version). Regardless, they apparently met little opposition and escaped in the taxi that had taken them there.[25] The whole time, Reggie "was quite unperturbed, and showed no reluctance to come with us," Florrie claimed.

If Reggie posed no problem, the promised car certainly did. It still wasn't there when they got back to their digs in Cardiff. There can be few things in life more stress-inducing than pulling off a spectacular crime like an armed kidnapping, only to have your getaway car fail to show up. The quartet moved to a new safe house, where they waited and sweated amid an intense police manhunt and heavy news coverage of the crime.

"The next two days strained all our nerves," Florrie said. "The car did not come and there was no information of any kind from either London or Manchester. The story appeared in the newspapers, prominently featured in the local ones. The taxi driver had been traced and had given what information he could."

Finally, the long-promised getaway car arrived—a taxi, piled with spare tires and gas tins. It was piloted by "a Russian-born Bolshevik who had been brought to London as a child, where he acquired an authentic cockney accent." Off they went, a motley revolution on wheels, headed for Manchester.

At some point in the middle of the night they were pulled over, and the Bolshevik got out to deal with the policeman. "He told the driver that he had only three front lights, apparently an offence then, and he should have had four," Florrie said. "The policeman asked for his driving license, discovered it had expired the previous midnight, and became more inquisitive."

An argument ensued between the driver and the policeman. Florrie was trying to stay out of it—there was a hue and cry out for the Irish kidnappers of a boy whose description matched the child with him, and he didn't want his accent adding to the copper's curiosity. As dismal situations involving the police go, this one could scarcely be made worse, but then the driver tried an age-old solution. He popped his head into the car and whispered, "give me a quid."[26] The IRA men coughed up the bribe, even as they sighed with relief. By 9 a.m. they were in Manchester and soon they would all be home.

Josephine put on a fine performance for a correspondent from the *Western Mail*, a Welsh newspaper, when she was interviewed about the kidnapping: "Oh, my darling boy! Is he dead or alive? What did they do it for? Why did they kidnap him, a harmless, innocent child?"

The correspondent, who described Josephine as a "pretty young woman," wasn't the only one she beguiled with her portrayal of a worried mother. Her interview ended thusly: "Mrs. Brown [*sic*] left with the intention of proceeding to the general commanding the Cork military at the barracks for his counsel and advice."[27]

By this point—December of 1920—it was becoming clear that General Strickland and Captain Kelly had a major leak on their hands inside Victoria Barracks. Just weeks before, on November 15, Josephine's information had gotten three British Army officers killed at Waterfall, outside Cork city. The kidnapping of her son made headlines across the British Isles. Scotland Yard was on the case—two detectives showed up in Cork. And yet apparently, inexplicably, Strickland and Kelly never seemed to connect Dot A (the intelligence leaks from their office) with Dot B (the kidnapping by Irish gunmen of their chief clerk's child, who was the subject of a custody battle).

Dealing with the security crackdown that followed the killing of the three British officers at Waterfall wasn't easy for Jo. Suspicions had in fact materialized—quite a few of her colleagues were dismissed and the British put her home under sporadic surveillance. It wasn't as easy to get documents out of Victoria Barracks, so Jo had to resort to memorizing material.[28]

But in April 1921, just weeks after Cruxy O'Connor gave away the Ballycannon safe house, Florrie and Jo got together once more in a church for the most consequential rendezvous of their lives—their wedding. It was done in secret, of course—Florrie was by now known to British intelligence and Jo was still working at Victoria Barracks. Swapping rings in a public ceremony was out of the question.

As late as May, she was still smuggling out material. As late as May, the British knew there was a major leak in Victoria Barracks. And as late as May, after all previous purges to plug that leak, they still hadn't prevented their chief clerk from passing vital secrets to her husband—the head of IRA intelligence in Cork.

"There was a case, in May of 1921, in which a document issued from British Sixth Division Headquarters, transmitted to Cork No. 1 Brigade by their operator there, was circulated, in part, and with some observations, to the Brigade Commandants," Florrie wrote. "A copy of the circular was captured by the British, again issued with their observations, and the new circular once more came into our hands."[29]

Jo deftly navigated the distorted mirrors, dark passages, and shifting floors of this espionage funhouse until the summer of 1921, when the British government and Irish republicans agreed on a truce. She ended her job at Victoria Barracks, but her intelligence work for the IRA didn't stop. There was a loose thread still to be tied up at Cobh, the port for Cork.

The loose thread's name was Paddy O'Connor.

"After the Truce, I went to Cobh with two members of the Brigade Intelligence Staff for the purpose of getting my sister, who was traveling to the U.S.A. to identify and ascertain the destination of a family named Connors or O'Connor," Jo said. "This family was going to the U.S.A. to join a member of it who had been in the IRA but who had given information to the enemy and had been got out of the country secretly by the British authorities. As a result of this action of my sister and myself, this man was traced by the IRA and subsequently shot in New York."[30]

Even as Florrie and Jo were getting married in April, the Irish American who would provide the guns for that shooting in New York was in the middle of a somewhat larger weapons procurement project for the IRA.

He was sitting, rather nervously, on a whole boatload of tommy guns.

Chapter 10

A Boatload of Tommy Guns

JIMMY MCGEE, A gunrunner and all-around fixer for the Irish Republican Army in New York, found himself in a fix in June of 1921.

There was a logistical problem: How do you get five hundred brand new tommy guns from the basement of a Catholic church in Manhattan onto a ship docked at an army base in Hoboken, New Jersey, past the police, the harbor patrol, the United States Army, federal Customs officials, the representative of the ship owner, and your own striking union that has picket lines up all over the New York waterfront?

And then there was a personnel problem: How do you get the ship's scab crew to quit so you can replace them with reliable Irishmen who can be counted on to say nothing about a secret cargo of Thompson submachine guns that could tilt the course of the Irish revolution?

As the secretary of the New York local of the marine engineers' union, McGee was leading a contract strike that had shut down much of New York harbor. But he was also a dedicated Irish revolutionary, and breathing down his neck was a blowtorch named Michael Collins—the leader of Ireland's fight for independence wanted those guns, and he wanted them yesterday.

As the IRA battled British forces from the rolling countryside of County Cork to the hills of Donegal, guns were in desperately short supply, and the outcome of the revolution hung in the balance. A big shipment of tommy guns from America could make all the difference for the rebels.

On the coast north of Dublin, the IRA was already burning down Coast Guard stations so the arms could be brought ashore without the British noticing. Collins ordered a top rebel officer in County Meath, Seamus Finn, to figure out where they could be landed. "One thousand Thompson guns had been purchased in America, and they were being met at sea by a yacht," Finn recalled.[1]

The number was off, but the logistical issues were the same.

So, strike or no strike, McGee had to get those guns to Hoboken and onto the *East Side*, the freighter that would carry them to Ireland. He seemed perfect for the job, an Irish-born, five-foot, ten-inch, two-hundred-and-forty-pound bulldog with a bent right pinky, broken in some old accident. "He was a great big man, a heavy man," said one IRA fighter who worked with him in New York.[2]

Normally McGee's position in the union helped grease the wheels for the rebels—he could get seaman's papers under false names for IRA men or talk Irish crew members into smuggling a few guns home for the cause. But the tommy gun shipment was the biggest assignment he had ever taken on, and instead of greasing the wheels, his role in the union was just so much sand in the gears. "McGee could not go near the piers on account of the strike," an associate said.[3] It's hard to stage-manage a production like this when you're not even supposed to be in the theater.

Before this drama was over, the Hoboken police would be facing off with federal Customs agents, the guns' manufacturer would be dragged into a major scandal, and a rising star in the Justice Department's Bureau of Investigation—a twenty-six-year-old named John Edgar Hoover—would be asking a lot of questions.

The whole thing got started six months before, in January 1921, when Collins saw a *Popular Mechanics* story about the new Thompson submachine gun.[4]

Invented by John T. Thompson, a retired US Army general, the gun that bears his name was designed for trench warfare—Thompson called it a "trench broom" for its ability to sweep dug-in positions with continuous fire.[5] Thompson founded the Auto-Ordnance Company of Hartford, Connecticut, to produce the weapon, but the war had ended by the time the first prototypes were ready. Without the prospect of huge military contracts, the startup company faced the prospect of failure. It needed a big customer, fast.

Enter the Irish Republican Army.

In a January 27, 1921, memo about the gun, Collins wrote "It looks like a splendid thing certainly," adding "I'd like to know what it costs."[6] The question of cost landed in the lap of the IRA's main fundraiser in America, Joseph McGarrity of Philadelphia. A native of County Tyrone in the north of Ireland, he emigrated to the United States at sixteen and soon became active in the Irish revolutionary organization Clan na Gael, the secret society that took over from the old Fenians as the US counterpart of the Irish Republican Brotherhood. As a businessman, McGarrity made and lost fortunes. As a revolutionary, he never lost sight of the bottom line.[7]

McGarrity started arranging some big orders from the Auto-Ordnance Company. The company was more than happy to oblige—it needed the money. And there may have been another reason—its main financial backer, the fabulously wealthy and aptly named Thomas Fortune Ryan, was a friend of de Valera and a supporter of Irish independence. Ryan first invested in Auto-Ordnance just a few months after the 1916 rising that nearly got de Valera executed.[8]

In January and April of 1921, orders for five hundred guns were placed by George Gordon Rorke and Frank Ochsenreiter, two law school buddies who were active in the cause of Irish independence. McGarrity also recruited a couple of Irish-born veteran US Army officers, Lieutenant Patrick Cronin and Major James Dineen, to demonstrate the weapon's power to Collins and the boys in Dublin.

The two got a helpful tutorial on the weapon from a salesman for the Auto-Ordnance Company, Owen Fisher, at the National Guard armory on Park Avenue in Manhattan.[9] They were soon off to Dublin with a few of the weapons. On May 24, 1921, Cronin and Dineen met Michael Collins and Richard Mulcahy, the IRA chief of staff, in an unoccupied house in the Dublin suburbs. Collins was accompanied by a few members of his special Dublin squad and by Tom Barry, the legendary rebel commander from West Cork. They all adjourned to the basement, where some bricks were set up against a wall as a target.

Collins and Mulcahy turned down an offer to test the gun, leaving the job to Barry, who was also a bit nervous. "Fearing that I would miss with this new-fangled gun and so let down West Cork in front of those GHQ and Dublin Squad officers I declined, but eventually took the gun, aimed, and with great luck smashed all the bricks to smithereens."[10]

Collins was duly impressed.

The money—$132,634—was handled by McGarrity and Harry Boland, the republican movement's special envoy to the United States. Ochsenreiter and Rorke, pretending to be sportsmen, acted as fronts for a third party, who went by Frank Williams.

Williams's real name was Laurence de Lacy—he was an Irish rebel wanted by the British on explosives charges.[11] After a 1915 raid on his home in Enniscorthy, County Wexford, turned up dynamite, blasting caps, and seditious literature, de Lacy made his way to America. He became an organizer for Clan na Gael.[12] Trusted by McGarrity, he was a natural for the tommy gun plot.

With the orders placed, the plotters had to figure out how to get the guns to Ireland. There was talk about moving them in small lots, but by late spring it was decided to gamble on one big throw of the dice—the guns would all go over in one shipload.

Over lunch, McGee warned Boland that such a large shipment would be very hard to handle. "I am forced to do this," Boland replied, citing pressure from Michael Collins. "The 'Big Fellow' is riding [expletive] out of me."[13]

The cover story was that the ship would carry a charity load of five thousand tons of American coal to help heat the homes of those in Dublin left destitute by the struggle for independence.[14] Beneath the coal there'd be enough weapons to warm the hearts of an army of revolutionaries.

Of course, for that much coal and that many guns, no small ship would do. This was where Jimmy McGee came in. He was the waterfront fixer, and if a ship was to be gotten, he was the man to do the getting. He initially had his eye on the *Ida*, which had been seized from Austria-Hungary during World War I. It was seaworthy and none too expensive, but the deal collapsed. Next, some of his co-conspirators chartered a ship in Baltimore, but McGee scotched the deal—his ability to fix things didn't extend that far. "We will have no control over the crew in Baltimore," he pointed out.[15]

And so, they settled on chartering the *East Side* out of New York. Owned by the Cosmopolitan Shipping Company, it was docked at West 9th Street. The crew hadn't joined the strike and getting them replaced by some reliable Irishmen was the first order of business. After a few beatings and death threats, the engine room crew decided they could live without the *East Side*.[16] Their departure didn't cause much of a stir—this was waterfront New York, and they were scabbing during a strike. It would have been strange if there had not been beatings and threats.

What did seem a little odd was the prompt arrival of a chief engineer who offered to take over and supply his own crew. Soon there were twenty new seamen aboard, and "many of them spoke with a strong Irish brogue," the *New York Times* reported.

The same trait that made the new crew members trustworthy for McGee—their ability to keep their mouths clamped shut as tight as a hatch in rough seas—made them seem furtive and clannish to the representative for the ship's owner. Fearing strike-related sabotage, he had the *East Side* moved across the harbor to the security of the US Army docks in Hoboken, which had been used as the embarkation point for troops headed to France in World War I.

The captain wouldn't be a problem. He was a pliable boozehound and whiskey smuggler who had just been caught with a thousand or so bottles on a run from France.

The guns were shipped by rail from the factory to New York, where Johnny Culhane picked them up at the American Rail Express Company and trucked them to a storehouse in the Bronx.[17] From there they headed to Manhattan—and the basement of a Catholic church on 29th Street.

The priests there were up to their clerical collars in gunrunning.

Irish rebel priests had existed for as long as rebels and priests had in Ireland. Among the New York clerics most active in gunrunning were the Carmelites, a religious order that dates back nearly nine hundred years. The Carmelites came to New York from Ireland in 1889 because the church needed help dealing with another sort of rebel priest—the Rev. Dr. Edward McGlynn.[18] The son of immigrants from County Donegal, McGlynn served in the 1880s as pastor of the largest parish in New York, St. Stephen's Church on East 28th Street, and he embraced the radical vision of the social reformer Henry George.

In 1886, George was the United Labor Party's candidate for mayor of New York, running on a heady brew of Irish nationalism and socialism—a combination that played well with McGlynn's working-class Irish parishioners, but it appalled both the church hierarchy and the Tammany Hall Democratic machine. When the Vatican excommunicated McGlynn over his outspoken support for Henry George, seventy-five thousand New Yorkers marched in protest.[19] To pacify McGlynn's Irish parishioners, Archbishop Michael Corrigan brought in Irish Carmelites, who set up a church near St. Stephens, Our Lady of the Scapular of Mount Carmel, and a priory at 338 East 29th Street.[20]

This did not exactly solve the rebel priest issue. Forty years later, the leader of the Carmelite order was the Most Rev. Peter Elias Magennis, who also happened to be a member of the Irish Republican Brotherhood.[21] Born in County Armagh, long a cauldron of sectarian tension, Magennis came to the United States in 1911 and took leading roles, public and private, in the republican movement.[22] Publicly, he led the Friends of Irish Freedom, which was founded in New York just weeks before the Easter Rising in 1916 to promote independence and raise money. Privately, he and his order provided the rebels with weapons and safe houses. "The New York Carmelites were involved in funding, purchasing and shipping arms to Ireland through the period 1916–1923," a historian for the order wrote.[23]

And Our Lady of the Scapular was smack in the middle of it. A longtime pastor of the church said that at one point before he arrived there, so many weapons were stored in the sacristy of the church that they threatened to break through the floor. They were moved to a windowless room in the basement.[24]

And the Carmelites were by no means the only priests aiding the effort to smuggle a few hundred tommy guns to Ireland. The Rev. Timothy J. Shanley worked tirelessly on the project. Born in County Leitrim, Shanley was the assistant pastor of St. Benedict the Moor Church, an African American parish in Hell's Kitchen, and a close associate of Irish republican leaders in New York.

He recalled how the crew of Irish seamen recruited by McGee showed up at the Carmelite priory to get the guns ready for shipment to the *East Side*: "The pieces had all been packed in burlap at 29th Street and sewed up by sailors."[25] The guns would be moved by truck from the priory to a motorboat, which would ferry them across the Hudson to the ship in Hoboken under cover of darkness. This was not the kind of cargo you listed on the ship's manifest.

The seamen loaded the truck, and some accompanied it across town to get the contraband cargo aboard the launch. The men had passed up other work for the *East Side* job, so they were happy to expedite matters, out of patriotism and weariness of sleeping on park benches—a shipless seaman was a homeless seaman. "We roamed around New York together with the sky as a roof and a copy of the *New York American* as a blanket to cover us at night in the park," recalled one of the crew, Larry Byrne.[26]

The quicker the *East Side* got under way, the quicker the crew would be off those park benches. But from the moment the launch pulled up alongside the *East Side*, in the wee hours of June 12, 1921, nothing went right. The burlap bags were transferred to the ship in the presence of the military officer in charge of the docks. The whole operation was also witnessed by officers of the nearby SS *McKeesport*.[27] Some crewmen hired by the ship's owners were looking on, too. Soon a couple of watchmen came on board, asking inconvenient questions about what came over the side from the launch.

The plan had been to get the bagged guns loaded into the cargo holds, cover the hatches and beat it on down to Norfolk, Virginia, where a load of coal would cover the contraband for the journey to Ireland. That was the plan, but McGee hadn't yet gotten rid of all the original crew, and the loaders couldn't get the guns down into the hold with them watching. Instead, the guns were taken down to the galley's refrigeration room—and a few were left outside. Now one of the watchmen was headed for the refrigeration room, which by this point amounted to one gigantic can of worms.

"One of them opened the door to the chill room," James Curley, the second assistant engineer, recalled. "I slipped the other one ten dollars and they both went away."[28]

The reprieve didn't last long. There were still a few burlaps bags outside the refrigeration room, and an assistant cook who wasn't in on the scheme got curious and pulled out a knife. He slit some burlap and got the surprise of his life when he spotted the muzzle of a Thompson. The next thing anyone knew, he was screaming about guns and that the whole crew was going to be murdered.

That got the watchmen back on board right quick.

The assistant cook took them down to the refrigeration room, and showed him the stuff, Curley said. "They opened three sacks to see what was in them."[29] Something had to be done, and fast. The solution: Another $10 bribe. It bought another reprieve, which allowed the men to move the stuff from the refrigeration room to the No. 4 hold. But the rivets were beginning to pop on this rust bucket of a plot—too many people had seen too much.

Some of the Irish crewmen went to McGee's home that night and told him the stuff should be pulled off the ship, but he was reluctant to act, saying he had done his part.[30] McGee had spent enough time at sea to know that when a ship is sinking, going back aboard rarely proves a wise move.

The crewmen were none too thrilled with McGee by this point. "The yellow S.O.B. was responsible for the loss of those guns," one recalled years later. That along with "dirty skunk" and "dirty rat" were among his kinder comments about McGee. Among his nastier ones: "If Magee had got what was coming to him, he would have been bumped off that time."[31]

Curley, the second assistant engineer who'd been so busy bribing watchmen on Sunday, caught a few hours' sleep, but at 10:30 a.m. the captain told him the ship was to be searched by US Customs for a mysterious cargo that had been put aboard the day before.[32]

This time the search couldn't be stopped with a $10 bribe. The Customs men came aboard Monday and searched and found nothing. The Irish crew, desperate to salvage the situation, found a tug and pulled up alongside the *East Side* on Monday night, determined to get the guns off. A watchman warned them off, threatening to blow them all to Davy Jones's locker (yes, he actually said that).[33] The men on the tug flashed badges and announced that they were Customs agents, but he still wouldn't budge, promising only to make a call to verify their identity. When he returned, the tug and the men were gone.

That incident only convinced the Customs people that there was something very fishy going on aboard the *East Side*, whose Irish crew was now vanishing as mysteriously as those burlap bags full of guns. On Tuesday, the day the ship was supposed to sail for Norfolk, the Customs men redoubled their efforts, searching the *East Side* from stem to stern. Nothing.

Too late to help McGee, the walkout that had so complicated the caper came to an end. Swallowing a 15 percent pay cut, the marine engineers' union voted that same day to end their strike. Maybe if it hadn't been for that mysterious tug incident the night before, the Customs men would have given up.

But on Wednesday, they searched again, and this time, they struck gold: nearly five hundred tommy guns, stashed in No. 4 hold.

The gunrunners weren't about to throw in the towel just because they'd been caught red-handed and Customs had confiscated the weapons. They quickly got to work on a political solution. Shanley reached out to Owen W. Bohan, an assistant district attorney in New York and prominent supporter of Irish independence. Together they called the Hoboken police chief, Patrick Hayes, who assured them that "he was as anxious as they were that the stuff might go over safely to Ireland, and he would cooperate."[34]

Looking for more political clout, Sean Nunan, an aide to de Valera who did fundraising in New York, contacted Eugene F. Kinkead. Born in Cork while his parents were visiting Ireland, Kinkead had quite a resume by that point: three-term Democratic congressman, sheriff of Hudson County, and a major in US Army intelligence in World War I.[35] A big supporter of Irish independence, he helped brainstorm a response.

The strategy was simple: "It was decided to make it a 'stolen property' job," Shanley recalled.[36] The story: Some nefarious thief had stolen those guns from their rightful owner, Frank Williams, and put them aboard the *East Side*. Now it was time for the police to step in and give Williams back what was properly his.

Kinkead "got in touch with the mayor of Hoboken, who was of Irish descent, as also was the chief of police of Hoboken, with the result that the Hoboken Police Department took the guns from the dock to police headquarters, on the grounds that the offence was committed in the state of New Jersey," Nunan said.[37]

The Customs men were none too happy when the police seized the guns they had just confiscated from the ship. As the holding cells at police headquarters overflowed with the weapons, the Customs men and the Hoboken coppers had it out until a judge in Newark stepped in. He settled matters by holding a hearing and awarding temporary custody to Customs.

Frank Williams had an interesting choice of attorney for the hearing— John J. Fallon, the counsel for the City of Hoboken. The city's Irish American governing elite was doing everything it could to help the IRA, which helps explain how fifty tommy guns managed to sprout legs and walk out the back door of Hoboken Police headquarters. Somehow, they made it back into the hands of the gunrunners.

The case mixed high drama and low farce. The man behind the tommy gun purchase, Frank Williams (aka Larry de Lacey), showed up at the scene, telling reporters he was a third character, Frank Kernan. That ruse collapsed when a Hoboken official walked up and said "Oh, Mr. Williams, just a moment."

Williams's lawyer, Thomas J. O'Neill, only added to the comedy when he was asked about his client's thick Irish accent. "An Irish brogue?" he responded. "Surely you mean a Canadian accent."[38]

You couldn't make this stuff up, and the newspapers went wild—the *East Side* was the lead story on the front page of the *New York Times* and the *Daily News*. "600 MACHINE GUNS SUPPOSED FOR IRISH TAKEN ON SHIP HERE," the *Times* declared (it was more like five hundred). The *Daily News* went with the dollar value: "$135,000 ARMS FOR ERIN SEIZED ON HOBOKEN PIER."

Soon, federal agents were hunting for the *East Side*'s engineering crew, which had largely jumped ship, and J. Edgar Hoover was interrogating officials of the Auto-Ordnance Company about exactly how its first big order ended up on the *East Side*.[39] Frank Ochsenreiter, the IRA front man, told Hoover he placed a February 15 order on behalf of his buddy, George Bordon Rorke, for a hundred guns at $180 each, plus ammo clips. At the time he placed the order, Ochsenreiter told Hoover, he was working for the Royal Typewriter Company—the man seemed to have an affinity for machinery that went rat-a-tat-tat.

Another name came up during the interview. Thomas Fortune Ryan was a major shareholder in Auto-Ordnance, Hoover learned.

An IRA attack in Dublin on June 16 added to the urgency of the investigation—a rebel with a tommy gun that had been smuggled in earlier opened up on a troop train at Drumcondra, spraying it with sixty bullets.[40] Other Volunteers hurled bombs and fired pistols. The British Army reported that one soldier was killed and two wounded in the splintered ruins of the train.

As the feds dug into the gunrunning case and tommy guns rattled Dublin, the *East Side*, amazingly, was allowed to sail for Norfolk—and it would seem there was still some contraband on board. One of the specially recruited Irish sailors recalled years later that another seaman, an associate of McGee, "dumped the stuff over the side at Sandy Hook."[41]

It was a good thing for the plotters that they deep-sixed the incriminating evidence—there were federal agents waiting when the ship docked in Norfolk. After an intensive three-month investigation, Rorke was charged in September with conspiracy and violations of the Neutrality Act. The government made clear in its case against the dapper twenty-nine-year-old Georgetown graduate that there were likely to be other defendants, and there were hints that "representatives of labor organizations" were involved.[42] That couldn't have done much for the sleep of Jimmy McGee. But Rorke walked free in November for lack of evidence.

And McGee wasn't included when a new round of federal indictments was handed down on June 19, 1922, nearly a year after the guns were found. Instead, the feds went after Marcellus Thompson, the vice president of Auto-Ordnance and the son of its founder.[43]

Among the charges against Thompson: "Conspiracy to set on foot and provide the means for a military enterprise to be carried on against the territory of a foreign prince with whom the United States was at peace."

In this case, the foreign prince happened to be none other than King George V of the United Kingdom, a kingdom that was soon to be less united, thanks to the sanguinary exertions of Thompson's customers. And in a highly unfortunate coincidence for the wedded bliss of the hapless Marcellus, fate had decreed that his father-in-law, George Brinton McClellan Harvey, would at that very moment be serving as the United States ambassador to Great Britain.

A *New York Times* headline writer with a keen feel for how to puncture the jugular emphasized the link in big front-page type: "HARVEY'S SON-IN-LAW HELD IN ARMS PLOT."

That the ambassador's daughter, Dorothy Harvey Thompson, had posed with a tommy gun in a publicity shot did nothing to mitigate the diplomatic damage. The simple fact was that her husband's company had sold guns to rebels who used them to freely splash British blood across Ireland.

Thompson, of course, attempted to deny the undeniable. He insisted he was shocked—shocked—to discover there was gunrunning involving his product: "Of course we would not think of selling to persons we might even suspect of reselling them into the hands of enemies of constituted governments." Some people might have believed him, but it appears that his wife was not one of them—their marriage never recovered. She headed off to Britain in 1923 and made her sympathies known by dancing with the future King George VI.[44]

Another apparent casualty of the scandal was her father's stint as ambassador to the Court of St. James. Harvey, who had been an adviser to President Woodrow Wilson, left the diplomatic service the year after his son-in-law's indictment.[45] A onetime managing editor of *Harper's Magazine*, he became the editor of the *Washington Post*.

Thompson was just the biggest name in the June indictments. Also charged were the Auto-Ordnance Company and its secretary, Frank J. Merkling, along with the customer/salesmen duo of Rorke and Ochsenreiter. The man behind the purchases, Frank Williams, aka Laurence de Lacy, went down, along with his brother, Fred Williams, aka Edward de Lacy. Both had already absconded to Ireland.[46] Bringing up the rear in the case was Johnny Culhane, the Bronx wheelman who had helped move the guns.

Announced with much fanfare, the case gradually fell apart. On January 22, 1923, the prosecution dropped the charges against the absent Frank Williams, and he was the linchpin of the conspiracy case. An important witness, Owen Fisher, had died, Irish American politicians like Kinkead were doing their best to bury the whole thing, and London didn't really care anymore—by now the Anglo-Irish war was over. Soon the other prosecutions shriveled and died on the vine.

Of course, that didn't mean the end to the legal battle. McGarrity and the republicans had shoveled a small mountain of money into the tommy gun deal, and they didn't plan on making their arsenal a gift to Uncle Sam. Frank Williams named McGarrity as his agent in the case, and McGarrity went to court and recovered the guns in November of 1925. American gun laws being what they were, it turned out that there was nothing illegal about buying five hundred machine guns to slaughter the armed forces of America's closest ally. McGarrity eventually got most of them to their intended destination (a few, it seems, were somehow diverted to 1930s American gangsters).[47]

As the *East Side* case wound down, J. Edgar Hoover's career geared up—he was named director of the federal Bureau of Investigation in 1924 and would spend a fair chunk of the next decade battling tommy-gun-toting criminals.

In Ireland, Thompson guns remained a part of the IRA's arsenal right into the 1970s and the Troubles in Northern Ireland.

It is perhaps fortunate for Cruxy O'Connor that those hundreds of guns from the *East Side* were in federal custody from June 1921 to November

1925. That meant there were none on hand in 1922, when the boys came back to Jimmy McGee with another weapons mission.

This time, it was nothing so complicated as moving a boatload of guns. This time, they just needed a few pistols, and there was no need to ship them to Ireland—the guns were needed for a job in New York.

This time, the IRA was coming to America.

Chapter 11

Passages

ONE STEP AHEAD of the IRA, Cruxy boarded the Cunard liner *Carmania* in Liverpool on June 30, 1921, accompanied by his brother, Michael F. O'Connor, who went by Frank. On the ship's manifest, Cruxy listed his occupation as accountant; his brother listed his as salesman.[1] Frank, two years younger, was temporarily leaving behind his wife, Florence, and his three-year-old son, John Patrick. They were bound for New York, hoping for a new life for the whole family beyond the reach of the Irish Republican Army.

In that, they couldn't have been more wrong.

The ship they boarded was, like Cruxy, a survivor—the *Carmania* had been pressed into service with the Royal Navy in World War I and took part in one of the conflict's most bizarre sea battles, sinking a German ship, the *Cap Trafalgar*, off Brazil in 1914. Both were converted ocean liners; the *Cap Trafalgar*, a German ship named after Britain's signature naval victory, had disguised itself as the *Carmania*, which wasn't taken in when they crossed paths. The title of a book about their naval duel captured its bizarre nature: *The Ship That Hunted Itself.*[2]

This voyage proved far less dramatic. The brothers arrived in New York harbor on August 8, and headed for a reunion with an aunt, Rosaleen Caffrey, of 308 East 66th Street, Manhattan. They had a lot to do—find work and an apartment, and get in touch with the family, who would be following them. The IRA had warned the remaining O'Connors, in the very clearest of language, that they were to clear out of Cork, quickly and forever.

Cruxy's betrayal of his comrades forced the family out of their longtime home in Mount Desert. They could hardly remain in a neighborhood that had lost six of its sons because of their son, especially with the Deasys right next door. The O'Connors took refuge at 7 Lancaster Quay in the center of Cork.[3] In late September, shadowed by Jo O'Donoghue's sister, they boarded the *Centennial State*, traveling in steerage to New York. There were four in all—Cruxy's parents, John and Hannah O'Connor, his sister-in-law, Florence O'Connor, and young John Patrick.

They arrived in New York harbor on October 2, unaware that they had left a trail that the IRA would follow. They disembarked in Hoboken, at the very same Army terminal where, less than four months earlier, five hundred tommy guns had been found aboard the *East Side*.

The O'Connors headed to the Upper West Side, and a reunion with Paddy and Frank. For the first time in months, they would all be back together again. They settled into an apartment at 483 Columbus Avenue, between 83rd and 84th Streets. Central Park beckoned, just a block away, if you needed a good stretch of the legs.

O'Connor found work as a bookkeeper at B. Altman's, the luxury department store that proudly occupied a block of Fifth Avenue from 34th to 35th Street. It was smack dab in the middle of Manhattan—so central a location that the Empire State Building would begin to rise diagonally across the street within a decade.

Of course, there was one big disadvantage to working in the heavily trafficked heart of Manhattan. As in London, it wasn't long before someone from back home in Cork spotted the informer.

The IRA Heads to New York

In late August 1921, with the cease-fire in effect, Dan Healy, still a nondrinker, was hanging out in a Cork pub with Martin Donovan and a few comrades from C Company. But Donovan had something other than rest and relaxation on his mind. Truce or no truce, the services that Healy specialized in were needed for some unspecified mission. "On leaving the premises, Martin Donovan called me to one side and told me he had a 'job' for me without mentioning what it was. Knowing Martin, as I did, I just said 'Okay.'"[4]

Three weeks or so later, the nature of the job became clear—in a matter of weeks, the long tentacles of IRA intelligence had latched onto O'Connor. As C Company held a training near Ballycannon, Pa Murray approached Healy with some news: "I had been chosen by the brigade to go to America to shoot the informer, Patrick Connors, then known to be in New York."

Healy later learned that when IRA commanders dropped the assignment in Donovan's lap, he was told that he could have any man he wanted for the job. To Donovan, the choice was clear, but it caused a bit of consternation in the upper echelons. Healy was by this point the head of the IRA's active service unit in Cork city, and the mission would put him out of the picture if the truce ended: "There were certain objections to my going, as it was feared that military operations would again commence and that I would be wanted here at home."

Healy and Donovan were briefed on the mission by the leaders of the Cork brigade—this would have included Florrie O'Donoghue, the brigade's intelligence chief, who had been tracking Cruxy. They were given general instructions, names to travel under, and information on how to contact Michael Collins, who would play a special role in the first leg of their journey.

"Martin Donovan and I went to Dublin and, after a considerable time, succeeded in contacting Mick Collins," Healy said. "It was decided that Martin and I should travel with Collins and his party, who were then going to London in connection with the truce negotiations. From my conversations with Collins, I gathered that our business in New York had the sanction of G.H.Q. [General Headquarters]. "[5]

Indeed, the funds for the trip came from the top echelon of the IRA.

That Collins would be conducting the treaty negotiations in London came as a surprise to a lot of people, not least Collins himself. De Valera had led a delegation that met with Prime Minister Lloyd George in July, after the truce took effect. It was assumed he would lead the treaty negotiations—after all, he had the Irish Parliament, or Dail, declare him the president of the Irish Republic in August.

Collins and nearly every other leader of the independence movement felt strongly that de Valera should lead the talks, but the president insisted on staying in Ireland "as the symbol of the Republic."[6] De Valera stood firm that Collins go in his place, a move that deeply troubled Collins. He poured out his misgivings to an aide, Batt O'Connor: "I will never forget his agony of mind. He would not sit down, but kept pacing up and down the floor, saying that he should not be put in that position; that it was an unheard-of thing that the soldier who had fought the enemy in the field should be elected to carry on negotiations. He said it was de Valera's job, not his."[7]

De Valera's insistence would have dire consequences for both Collins and the new nation, but it got Donovan and Healy into England.

In London, Healy obtained a passport under the name Thomas O'Dwyer, of 14 High Street, Newry, County Down.[8] Claiming he was heading to New

York for a vacation, he got a US visa with the help of Eamon Broy, a close aide to Collins who had served as his spy within the Dublin Metropolitan Police.

Donovan struck out when he tried the same tack. He visited passport offices all over England and got nowhere. Finally, he stowed away on an ocean liner out of Liverpool, where the IRA had impeccable waterfront connections.

Pa Murray, who had joined the pair in London, had no better luck than Donovan. Turned down in his efforts to get a passport, he sought help from a London IRA man named Shanahan who was practiced in the art of greasing wheels and palms: "I believe that Shanahan bribed some British official to secure the necessary passport," Healy recalled.

And so, the three were on their way, on a hunt for O'Connor that Florrie O'Donoghue acknowledged was extraordinary. "At a time when every man and every shilling was needed, we went to the trouble and expense of sending three men after him to America."[9]

But to what end?

The IRA had thrice tried to kill O'Connor, with poison at Victoria Barracks, with an ambush at the Blarney train station, and with a stakeout at the Hammersmith Post Office. It would have been perfectly understandable to give up once the man was out of the British Isles and no longer posed any kind of direct threat. So why go to all the trouble of mounting a fourth attempt at great expense a continent away, in a city central to IRA fundraising and public relations, with some of the most valuable men in this secret army?

"Secret" may hold the key. The IRA liked to think of itself as an army, but for all the talk about brigades and battalions and flying columns engaging crown forces in open battle, it remained in many ways a secret society writ large, a guerrilla force that could survive only if it swam in a sea of secrecy. Informers were the single biggest threat to that secrecy, even more so than outside spies who tried to infiltrate an area. Florrie O'Donoghue illuminated the distinction.

"Looking at the facts, I could not see spies being successful against the tight organization we had then," he recalled, pointing out that IRA men tended to know each other personally. "The man who could horn in would need to be a genius. Traitors and informers were a more dangerous possibility."[10]

Traitors and informers were more dangerous because they possessed an insider's knowledge of names and places—knowledge that it would take an outside spy months or years to attain. And that information could wreak havoc. The Ballycannon massacre was the worst blow that crown forces inflicted on the Cork city IRA.

Paddy O'Connor hadn't just betrayed his comrades and his country—he had betrayed the community that nurtured him and he had gotten away with it. He needed to pay and be seen to pay for what he'd done—not just as punishment, but as a warning to others who might be tempted to follow suit. That's why the IRA often put signs on the bodies of the those they executed as traitors, labeling them as spies or informers.

And so, Paddy had to die, even if it took a trip to America by a trio of Cork's top gunmen to do it.

This wouldn't be the first time vengeance was taken against an Irish informer thousands of miles away. An earlier case involved two of the most spectacular assassinations in modern Irish history—and Sherlock Holmes.

On May 5, 1882, London's newly appointed chief secretary for Ireland, Lord Frederick Cavendish, had been in the country for a mere matter of hours. He was walking near his new home in Phoenix Park with his top aide, Thomas Burke, the undersecretary, when several men with long surgical knives attacked them. In a matter of minutes, Cavendish and Burke were dead, their blood staining the grass of that vast green expanse in Dublin.[11]

The butchery stunned the world.

Dublin detectives quickly rounded up the members of an Irish Republican Brotherhood splinter group, the Invincibles, and one of the conspirators, James Carey, was caught in the dragnet. He talked to save his neck, and five of his accomplices swung from the gallows. Now the authorities had to get Carey and his family out of the British Isles, and so he, his wife, and their seven children were sent to South Africa. On July 29, 1883, they were on the coastal steamer *Melrose* when Carey was gunned down by Patrick O'Donnell, a native of Gweedore, County Donegal.[12]

O'Donnell had an interesting resume that included links to the American branch of a violent Irish secret society, but it wasn't Clan na Gael or the Fenians. It was the Molly Maguires of the Pennsylvania anthracite region, where he and his family had emigrated. During the Great Famine, the Mollies had gained notoriety in the Ulster borderlands by attacking land-lords who evicted tenant farmers, leaving them to starve. When poverty, discrimination, and political repression turned the hard-coal region of Pennsylvania into another Ulster for Irish Catholics, the Mollies were resurrected, this time to fight the coal companies that ruled the region with a rod of iron.[13]

And the O'Donnell family was in the thick of it.

Two of Patrick O'Donnell's cousins, Charles and James "Friday" O'Donnell, were implicated in a notorious Molly crime, the double murder of a mine boss and his friend on September 1, 1875. Vigilantes, almost certainly acting on information from a Pinkerton spy who had infiltrated the Mollies, invaded the O'Donnell home in Wiggans Patch, Schuylkill County, on December 10, 1875, and fatally shot Charles and his pregnant sister, Ellen McAllister. Jack Kehoe, the husband of another O'Donnell cousin, was reputed to be the leader of the Mollies in Schuylkill County. He was convicted and hanged for the 1862 killing of a mine boss, a murder he probably didn't commit, after the secret society was broken by the Pinkerton spy, James McParlan.

Patrick O'Donnell himself was accused of being a leader of the organization. "He is the man I knew in the Pennsylvania coal regions," a letter writer told the *Post-Express* of Rochester, New York, after the Carey murder. "He was the chief of the Molly Maguires then."[14]

O'Donnell invoked the violence of the Pennsylvania coal fields in testifying that he acted in self-defense when he killed Carey: "I come from a part of America where people don't want to inquire into a man's intentions when his pistol is against your forehead."

Given the fate of the O'Donnell family in Pennsylvania, Patrick clearly had no love for informers and spies. Carey's wife testified that O'Donnell told her "I was sent to do it" after the killing. Others heard "I had to do it," so whether O'Donnell acted on his own initiative or on behalf of an organization remains unclear. He was hanged on December 18, 1883.

Years later, William Pinkerton of the famed detective agency met Arthur Conan Doyle on a trans-Atlantic voyage and related the story of the Mollies and Patrick O'Donnell.[15] It served as the basis for Conan Doyle's Sherlock Holmes novel, *The Valley of Fear*, which involved a violent secret society in the mining regions of America, and the murder a continent away of the spy who brought it down.

In Conan Doyle's next work, "His Last Bow" (1917), Holmes impersonated an embittered Irish American who joined a secret society and traveled across the Atlantic to Cork, where he "gave serious trouble to the constabulary in Skibbereen."[16] A deal to film it had already been signed when three Cork members of the Irish Republican Brotherhood headed in the opposite direction to create some serious trouble for the constabulary in New York.

Danny Healy was the first to arrive, landing in New York on February 4, 1922. He immediately got in touch with Gilbert Ward, a member of the

Irish Mission to the United States, handing him a letter of introduction from Michael Collins and explaining his mission.[17] Two or three weeks later, Martin Donovan arrived, and shortly thereafter, Pa Murray showed up. Healy and Donovan found a place to stay on Lexington Avenue—Murray preferred his own company and would rendezvous with the pair each day.

Now all they had to do was find one man in a city of 5.6 million.

Chapter 12

The Hunt

THE ROARING TWENTIES city that was their hunting ground resembled nothing Murray, Donovan, and Healy had ever seen—the latter marveled at the crowds in Times Square. New York's industry was sprawling; its diversity, stunning; its entertainment, sizzling; and its criminality, shocking.

The port handled half of America's international trade, and New York's factories produced one-twelfth of everything manufactured in the United States.[1] About 35 percent of New Yorkers had been born abroad—479,797 in Russia, 390,832 in Italy, 203,450 in Ireland, 194,154 in Germany, and 145,679 in Poland.[2]

Babe Ruth was dazzling Yankees fans at the Polo Grounds, and Louis Armstrong was providing a soundtrack for the Harlem Renaissance. Prohibition had begun in 1920, spawning underworld wars involving an army of colorfully named gangsters, from Lucky Luciano to Bugsy Siegel to Vincent "Mad Dog" Coll—the latter, like Patrick O'Donnell, a product of Gweedore, Ireland.

Were a teenage Coll as adept as O'Donnell at spotting informers far from home, Murray, Donovan, and Healy could have used his help. The trouble was that the three were much better at shooting policemen than they were at playing detective. They were essentially running a missing persons case, but they initially proved as inept at finding O'Connor as he was at hiding himself.

Danny Healy did some initial scouting while he waited for Murray and Donovan to arrive and got precisely nowhere.

The IRA knew from Jo O'Donoghue's sister that the O'Connor family had sailed for New York—it had even tracked down the address of Cruxy's aunt on 66th Street, either from a passenger manifest or by monitoring the O'Connors' mail. The focus narrowed a bit further when Teddy Courtney, an engineer at the Ford factory in Cork, passed along a juicy tidbit from a lady friend in New York. The friend, a Miss Conway, had learned that O'Connor was working at the B. Altman department store, his experience at Roches in Cork having come in handy.

The New York–bound gunmen met with Courtney before leaving Cork, then paid a visit to Conway when they arrived there. Soon they were staking out the department store, but it seems they hadn't learned a key lesson of surveillance—the need to be inconspicuous. "The three of us set out to watch Altman's," Healy said. "One evening about 6 o'clock when Altman's workers were going home, 'Pa' spotted Connors leaving the store with the others. We followed him for a short distance but lost touch with him."[3]

Even as Murray spotted Cruxy, O'Connor must have seen him, because he stopped showing up for work.

That didn't stop the boys from continuing the stakeout. They kept a constant and fruitless watch on the department store. With every day that went by without a glimpse of their prey, the frustration mounted. Danny Healy, for one, bitterly lamented that they weren't getting the kind of help they had been promised by Michael Collins.

"I remember Collins saying that he had 'Some very good men in New York,'" Healy said. "By this I took him to mean that we would be afforded every assistance when we got there. In fact, the contrary was the case."[4]

In fact, Collins did have some good men in New York—they were just occupied with matters a trifle more pressing than eradication of stool pigeons. In addition to the vital tasks of raising money for and seeking recognition of an independent Ireland, they were dealing with the fallout of de Valera's recent trip to the United States.

The president of the Irish Republic had created a civil war in Irish America.

The New York Office

Essentially the split came down to de Valera and the Irish Republican Brotherhood vs. the longtime leaders of the IRB's American cousin, Clan na Gael. For decades there had been an understanding between the two organizations—the IRB decided how best to handle matters on its patch of turf, Ireland, while the Clan ran things in America.[5]

Just weeks before the Easter Rising, the secretive Clan had created a public organization, the Friends of Irish Freedom, to push the cause of independence. When the rising collapsed, the new organization wrung every drop of propaganda it could from the execution of leaders like Pearse and Connolly.[6] It arranged American speaking tours for prominent Irish proponents of independence and raised $100,000 to relieve suffering in Ireland.

This division of labor and turf worked just fine until a situation arose that no one could have imagined—de Valera, the leader of the Irish Parliament, or Dail Eireann, came to the United States in the summer of 1919 and stayed, for a full year and a half. The move, which came just as the war for independence was heating up, was designed to seek recognition of the Irish Republic, and money to fund it.

For de Valera, the passage to America was humbling—he stowed away on the *Lapland* out of Liverpool "dressed as a sailor in overalls and an old cap."[7] Before the ship left port, he had to hide in an unused tank, a couple of sandwiches stuffed in his overcoat pockets, while the authorities searched the ship for a murder suspect.

That would have been bad enough, but according to one story, de Valera wasn't alone in the tank. When a sympathetic crew member checked on him and asked how he was faring, he responded: "All right, only for the rats. They've eaten the sandwiches out of my pockets."[8]

When the ship reached New York, de Valera disembarked in his old sailor's clothes. His first stop was telling: the Carmelite priory on 29th Street. From there he headed to Philadelphia to spend some time with Joe McGarrity, the republican movement's main money man in America.

Finally, de Valera made a public appearance, a grand banquet in the splendor of the Waldorf Astoria at 33rd and Fifth Avenue—a stone's throw from B. Altman's. The tony hotel would be his headquarters for the remainder of his long stay in America, and it was there that he was greeted by two men who began as allies and ended as enemies, John Devoy and Judge Daniel Cohalan.

Devoy was an old rebel from County Kildare who'd done years in prison for treason after forming IRB circles within the British Army. Upon release in 1871 he was exiled to the United States, where he dedicated his life to journalism and the cause of a free Ireland. His newspaper, the *Gaelic American*, served as a soapbox for the Irish cause and for whatever political grudges Devoy was pursuing—Woodrow Wilson was a frequent target. Devoy's partner in the struggle was Judge Daniel Cohalan, an American-born lawyer who went from Grand Sachem of the Tammany Society to justice on the New York Supreme Court.[9] (The Tammany position was the more exalted one—in New York, the Supreme Court is where trials are held.)

As well as they all got along that night at the Waldorf Astoria, differences soon emerged between the two camps. The fight focused on money, turf, and principle. An American-born Irishman, de Valera expected deference and dollars from Irish-born Americans. An Irish-born American, Devoy expected de Valera to defer to the locals' expertise in American politics. When Devoy and Cohalan wanted to use money raised for the Irish cause to campaign against Woodrow Wilson, de Valera reacted like they were rats eating the sandwiches out of his pockets. Snubs and snide remarks added to the ill will. At one point toward the end of 1919, de Valera wrote that, "as big as this country is, it is not big enough to hold the Judge and myself."[10]

An IRA man on the run who was helping out in the New York office summed up Devoy's Clan na Gael this way: "Despite all the talk at their meetings of fighting for Ireland's freedom and all that kind of thing, the organization as such seemed to concern itself more with political matters than with any practical efforts to help to carry on the fight in Ireland." He seemed surprised that Clan na Gael members considered themselves "American citizens first and last," and could not understand their reluctance to violate US law by running guns to Ireland.[11]

De Valera did not lack allies among the Irish Americans. If Devoy and Cohalan made a formidable pair, so did two men who backed de Valera— McGarrity, and his compadre from Carrickmore, County Tyrone, Patrick McCartan, who had been the Dublin correspondent for Devoy's *Gaelic American*.[12]

The differences came to a head with the 1920 presidential campaign. Devoy and Cohalan hoped to convince the Republican Party to add a plank to its platform favoring the right of the Irish people to freely determine their own government. The mild wording was strategic—the pair figured that was the most they could get from the Republicans, and that the Democrats would then have to take up the issue as well.[13] And they might have pulled it off, were it not for de Valera. He showed up in Chicago for the Republican convention and issued a statement accusing Devoy and Cohalan of undermining his efforts to secure recognition for the Irish Republic. He pushed a more strongly worded resolution that had no chance of adoption and undermined his rivals. In the end, the Republican Party platform said nothing about Ireland.[14]

Even some of de Valera's supporters were shocked by the blatant attempt by a foreign leader to openly interfere in American politics. Perhaps as an American citizen, de Valera felt that what he was doing did not amount to interference, but he wasn't acting as an American citizen. He was acting as the leader of Ireland.

The growing strains finally reached a breaking point in October, when the Irish Republican Brotherhood split from the Devoy-dominated Clan na Gael, blaming Cohalan and Devoy's newspaper, the *Gaelic American*.[15]

De Valera finally returned to Ireland in mid-December 1920, right around the time that Paddy O'Connor was executing a suspected spy in Cork. He left trusted aides behind to clean up the mess in America.

A rival Clan na Gael had to be sown and nurtured—the reliable Jimmy McGee was named treasurer in 1922.[16] Likewise, a replacement had to be found for the Friends of Irish Freedom, which de Valera had not managed to wrest from Devoy and Cohalan. Thus was born the American Association for the Recognition of the Irish Republic, which could be counted on to follow de Valera's lead.

The cleanup crew consisted of men like Harry Boland, Sean Nunan, and Gilbert Ward, who had greeted Healy. Boland, the head of the Irish Republican Brotherhood, had been de Valera's advance man in America and stayed on as his special envoy, based in Washington. Nunan, like Boland a veteran of the Easter Rising, was de Valera's personal secretary in America, and stuck around in New York to raise funds for the Irish Republic and run guns for the IRA. Nunan had a special $100,000 slush fund "for the purchase and shipment of arms."[17]

Helping Nunan was Edmond O'Brien, an IRA man who had to flee County Limerick after a bloody shootout with the police on a train. Now he was up to his neck in gunrunning, which made him a regular visitor to the Carmelite priory on 29th Street. He'd head to a munitions factory outside New York, pay in cash for a few thousand rounds of ammunition, then return to Manhattan. "One of the priests there had the back entrance opened promptly on our arrival, so that we could drive straight in and dump our load without delay," he recalled.[18]

With Prohibition in effect, these trips could be risky: "Suspicious-looking cars were always liable to be held up and searched for contraband liquor." O'Brien fought fire with fire: He got a sympathetic Irish American cop named Chris Lynch to ride shotgun.

"He was in uniform and sat with me in the front of the car with his handcuffs on his lap," O'Brien recalled. "The idea was that, if there was any police holdup of traffic, which was of frequent occurrence then because of the operation of the Volstead Act (Prohibition), he would snap the other side of the handcuffs on to my wrist to indicate that I was in custody as his prisoner. This would give us a free pass through any police cordon."[19]

One time O'Brien and Dick O'Neill, a seaman who helped ship the stuff to Ireland in small lots, were moving a load of 17,000 rounds of ammunition without Lynch when they ran into trouble at a traffic light on the West Side of Manhattan. "While we were stopped there, two detectives, who were on the sidewalk, crossed over to the car and, seeing the parcels in the back of it, ordered us to pull onto the sidewalk," O'Brien said. "We had no alternative but to obey, of course, but, knowing as I did how favorably disposed to our cause most of the New York police were, I was under the impression that we would be allowed to proceed once matters were explained. But this time we had happened to hit the wrong one."

The officer in charge was Polish American.

He took a dim view of carloads of bullets, and literally blew the whistle, which brought half a dozen patrolmen running. O'Brien and O'Neill were hauled off to the station house, where they were taken to a basement interrogation room and subjected to the third degree by a squad of plainclothes officers. The pair admitted the obvious but gave a stand-up performance.

"We accepted full responsibility for the stuff, not concealing the fact that we were sending it to Ireland, but we insisted that we were acting entirely on our own and refused to implicate anyone else," O'Brien said.

The boys were booked, bundled into a police wagon and trundled off to the Tombs, the municipal jail in Lower Manhattan, where they were fingerprinted and assigned to different cells. The Tombs was connected to the criminal courts building, and as the pair were hauled before a judge that night, their prospects appeared bleak. The prosecution had plenty of ammunition—a carload, in fact.

But the law worked in mysterious ways when Irish gunrunners got caught red-handed in the New York area. In this case, an old neighbor of O'Brien's from County Limerick happened to witness his arrest. "He saw us being handcuffed and put into the police wagon, and immediately sent word through some friends of the Irish cause to Harry Boland and Sean Nunan to let them know what had happened," O'Brien said. "They apparently made contact with some of the sympathetic police officials they were in touch with, and so, when we were brought before this court, the procedure was the merest formality. I forget what the charge was that was brought against us, but it was something trivial. We were fined a dollar each and released immediately."[20]

As O'Brien and O'Neill slipped out a side door, they were met by several Irish American policemen who apologized for their Polish American colleague. He didn't know "his business," they said.

Oh, and about those 17,000 rounds of ammunition? Well, of course they could be returned to their rightful owners for use against one of America's closest allies. The helpful and friendly officers at the courthouse door gave "us a phone number to ring so that they would have the stuff waiting when we called," O'Brien said.

O'Brien also got pulled into some risky counterintelligence operations. In early 1920, Harry Boland came to him with a special job involving a British intelligence agent who was registered at a hotel in New York: "My mission was to impersonate the agent and try to obtain some more information in that way."[21]

O'Brien checked in to the Breslin Hotel under the name the British agent was using, A. D. Pate, and collected his mail. He instructed the staff to send up to the room any correspondence that arrived during the night, and by morning had half a dozen letters and telegrams. There wasn't much point in hanging around—the real Mr. Pate might show up at any moment, so O'Brien left, and took a circuitous route to meet Boland, who promptly went to work opening and deciphering the spy's messages.

They struck the mother lode.

"The gist of them was that this British agent had been authorized by his government to recruit gunmen and thugs in America for employment in Ireland against the IRA," O'Brien said, adding. "No British government department would have to accept responsibility for them or for their actions. There was a figure mentioned as rate of pay, which I think amounted to about £8 or £9 per week, for any men who would carry out the work required. In plain terms, these men were to act as paid assassins."[22]

Boland killed the assassin plot by leaking it to a radical newspaper.

And speaking of assassins—O'Brien was just the kind of man who might have proven invaluable to Pa Murray and Company once they landed in Manhattan. He knew how to use a gun, he knew how to use his head, and he'd been around the block a few times in New York. But by the time they showed up, he had moved to Chicago, where his wife's family had relatives. (There he had a chance to get to know Dineen and Cronin, the Irish-born US Army officers who were soon to head off to Ireland to demonstrate the power of the Thompson gun.)

That left the boys in the gnarled hands of Jimmy McGee, who Danny Healy said provided "the greatest possible help." Healy was not exaggerating. One IRA man described the O'Connor job this way: "All the crowd in New York were talking, but there was only one, Jimmy McGee, who was willing to do the shooting."[23]

Of course, that wouldn't be necessary with experienced gunmen like Murray, Donovan, and Healy on hand. McGee did help in other ways, though. In addition to providing the trio with revolvers, he was mixed up in some much bigger arms procurement projects with Murray. It seems that Pa had temporarily picked up some of O'Brien's duties in that department. And McGee knew plenty of merchant seamen willing to smuggle weapons into Ireland.

"I sent a terrible lot of stuff to Cork through Jimmy McGee," Murray recalled.[24]

Healy and Donovan focused their efforts on trying to track O'Connor. After the stakeout at B. Altman's proved fruitless, they realized that they needed to try a different tack. Finally, Healy came up with a brainstorm— one that would have occurred to any rookie cop in about three seconds: "I remember getting what turned out to be a brainwave when I suggested going to Connors' old 'digs' at night, where, with a bit of luck, we might be fortunate enough to get his new address. (We had been given his old address before leaving Ireland). We were lucky as we got the new address."

The stakeout moved to the Upper West Side.

"A few nights later, when keeping watch on the new address, I 'ran into' Frank Connors, a brother of Paddy's (our man)," Healy said. "We then knew we were on the right trail."[25]

And it was clear to Healy that Cruxy knew they were right on his tail. "We kept a constant watch on the block of flats where Paddy Connors lived with his brother and saw him leave the house on succeeding nights," he recalled. "We noticed that every night we saw him leave the house he went in a different direction."

Central Park appeared to be a favorite destination.

"On one occasion we trailed him, Martin and 'Pa' going one way, but I, anticipating his move, went in another direction and came almost face to face with him on the footpath," Healy said. "I was unarmed on this occasion, as were 'Pa' and Martin. However, I kept track of Connors and saw him go in the direction of a cinema."

About a week later they returned, armed with revolvers supplied by McGee. O'Connor came bounding down the steps of the apartment building, out into the fresh breezes of an April eve, headed for the park.

Within minutes, he'd be crumpled on the steps of the Semple School for Girls, bullet-riddled, bleeding, and all but dead.

The Ballycannon boys, slaughtered on Spy Wednesday, had been avenged on Holy Thursday.

Chapter 13

▟▟▟

The Heel of the Hunt

MURRAY, DONOVAN, AND Healy got away with it, with a little help from some friends.

The investigation into the O'Connor ambush went nowhere, and not just because the victim clammed up. The word was that de Valera had a man in the district attorney's office who put the kibosh on the case.[1] The prosecutor was Owen W. Bohan, who had so helpfully talked the Hoboken police chief into confiscating those tommy guns from Customs agents during the *East Side* fiasco. Bohan came up through the Tammany machine, an ally of midtown's Thomas J. McManus, or "The McManus" as he was styled in the manner of the old Irish clan chieftains.

In 1905, Bohan helped The McManus supplant Tammany's infamous George Washington Plunkitt from a Democratic leadership position.[2] Plunkitt, a product of a pre–Central Park settlement of African Americans and Irish immigrants on the very spot where Cruxy was shot, literally redefined corruption.[3] It was he who gave the world the memorable phrase "honest graft," and he was perfectly honest about his dishonesty: "I seen my opportunities and I took 'em."[4]

After a few terms in the state assembly, Bohan was appointed an assistant district attorney in 1916. By the early 1920s he was also neck deep in the Irish republican cause in New York. Jimmy McGee's daughter said that Bohan used his clout to ensure the trio from Cork weren't caught: "The matter was quashed."[5]

117

While the investigation stalled, the gunmen went on an East Coast tour.[6] First they took a weekend trip to Boston, to see Pa Murray's uncle. Then they headed down to Philadelphia to see Joseph McGarrity. McGarrity was born in County Tyrone, and settled in Philadelphia, a magnet for Ulster Catholic immigrants. His house on Springfield Avenue was a regular stopping place for leading republicans—when Healy and Donovan visited him, they were following in the footsteps of Pearse and de Valera.

The McGarrity visit was a risky move—Healy and Donovan were not politicians like de Valera. They were gunmen in a recent crime committed on American soil. The minute they met up with McGarrity, they made the IRA's most valuable ally in the United States an accomplice after the fact to a sensational felony in a state that bordered Pennsylvania.

And by now investigators knew Healy's identity. Cruxy may not have talked, but his brother Frank had run into the triggerman while he was staking out the O'Connor apartment. It was time to head home to Cork.

Somebody scrounged up some British passports under false names and they booked passage on the *Mauritania* in late April. It looked like smooth sailing until a predeparture meeting at Jimmy McGee's place with Liam Pedlar and Gilbert Ward. They had some bad news for Healy.

"It was stressed by McGee, Pedlar, and Ward that I should not travel on the *Mauritania* as it was understood that the American authorities knew my proper name," Healy recalled. "I protested, because I was travelling under another name (O'Dwyer) not known (so far as I was aware) to the Americans."[7] In the end, Healy reluctantly agreed to skip the voyage, and Donovan decided he could not in good conscience proceed without him—"as he and I had started out on this job together, we would see it out to the finish together."

Pa Murray went ahead on the *Mauritania* while McGee arranged for Healy and Donovan to stow away on the *St. Louis* bound for Hamburg. They went aboard pretending to be firemen who'd feed the boilers. But they never had to shovel any coal—they were not among the listed crew. "It was not too difficult to escape detection as these big liners carried a large number of firemen who worked in three shifts," Healy said. "For this reason, the engineer in charge of one shift would not know the men working with another engineer on a different shift."

They scrounged around for bunks—at one point they were bounced from some hospital beds. And Donovan, the scourge of the Royal Irish Constabulary, did a wee bit of detective work, aiding a search for whiskey that had been stolen from some passengers.[8] By May they were in Hamburg, where they jumped ship to the London-bound *Barbadian*, again stowing away with the aid of some sympathetic countrymen. Britannia may have ruled the waves, but Erin had thoroughly infiltrated the ships and the docks.

The accommodations on the *Barbadian* were every bit as luxurious as the ones de Valera enjoyed on his cruise to America—Healy and Donovan had to climb aboard on a rope, like rats, and were temporarily stashed in a compartment where the bosun's stores were kept. From there they were downgraded to the coal bunkers, where they remained hidden until they reached London, fed by a friendly Welsh crew member. When the ship docked in the Thames, they shook the coal dust from their clothes and snuck off the ship. By the end of May, they were back in Cork.

Pa Murray had an easier time of it. When the *Mauritania* docked, he met Reggie Dunne, who led the IRA in London, and Joe O'Sullivan, who had seen off Dan Healy the previous winter. The pair had some interesting news—they had a mission not unlike the one Murray had just completed. They were going to assassinate Field Marshal Henry Wilson, the head of the British Army at the end of World War I. The product of an Anglo-Irish landlord family in County Longford, Wilson had threatened to resign just before the war when the government was considering a crackdown on the Ulster Volunteers. After the war he served as a security consultant for newly minted Northern Ireland.

And from what Dunne and O'Sullivan told Murray, the job had been authorized from on high. "The shooting of Henry Wilson was official," Murray said. "Collins knew of it and Sam Maguire also."[9]

And it would soon plunge the trio of New York gunmen into a new war. An Irish civil war.

The Split

The secret army that had hunted O'Connor through three countries began tearing itself apart—along with all of Ireland—even as the fusillade that brought him down was echoing off the facades of Central Park West. O'Connor was shot about 8:30 p.m. on April 13. In Dublin, hours ahead of New York, it was early Friday morning, and a hardline faction of those in the IRA who opposed the treaty Collins had helped negotiate with Britain were at that very moment taking the first step toward civil war, seizing Dublin's judicial center, the Four Courts.[10]

Just six years before, Irish republicans intent on a blood sacrifice to resurrect the Irish nation seized the General Post Office in the Easter Rising. Now, die-hard IRA men who refused to sacrifice their clear vision of an independent republic for the misty promise of an Irish Free State were trying something very similar—on Good Friday.

There is a significance in dates.

The split centered on the treaty that de Valera had insisted Collins help negotiate instead of himself. De Valera was unhappy with the deal Collins and Arthur Griffith, the minister of foreign affairs, hammered out with Lloyd George and Winston Churchill. The treaty called for the withdrawal of British troops and created an Irish Free State with dominion status, like Canada. Ireland would be ruled by the Irish.

But government officials would be required to take an oath to "be faithful to His Majesty King George V, his heirs and successors." And the treaty effectively recognized the likely creation of two Irelands—the largely Catholic Free State in the south and a predominantly Protestant Northern Ireland, which would remain a part of the United Kingdom and encompass six of the island's thirty-two counties.

The Irish side didn't swallow the compromises easily. As Churchill put it: "Michael Collins rose looking as if he was going to shoot someone, preferably himself. In all my life I have never seen so much passion and suffering in restraint."[11]

As far as Collins was concerned, he had gotten what could be gotten. The important thing, he said, was that Ireland now had the freedom to achieve freedom.[12]

When he signed the treaty in the wee hours of December 6, 1921, Collins knew that there was a very personal price to be paid: "When you have sweated, toiled, had mad dreams, hopeless nightmares, you find yourself in London's streets, cold and dank in the night air. Think—what have I got for Ireland? Something which she has wanted these past 700 years. Will anyone be satisfied with the bargain? Will anyone? I tell you this—early this morning I signed my own death warrant."[13]

As far as de Valera was concerned, Collins and company had betrayed the republic. After all the sweat and toil, after all the blood and tears, Ireland still would not be an independent republic. And the island would be partitioned, with the United Kingdom keeping northeast Ulster. De Valera damned the treaty as "the most ignoble document that could be signed" and accused the negotiators of exceeding their authority.[14] But his cabinet approved the deal, and on January 7, 1922, the Dail passed it by a vote of sixty-four to fifty-seven.

De Valera resigned as president the next day, to be replaced by Arthur Griffith.

The split reverberated through February, spreading to the Irish Republican Brotherhood. Through March, the nation drifted toward civil war. The IRA divided, the protreaty Free Staters vs. the antitreaty rebels.

In April, the guns came out. Antitreaty IRA men, cut off from government funding, began holding up banks. On April 14, they seized the Four Courts, even as Cruxy O'Connor was being gunned down in New York. Two days later, on Easter Sunday, shots were fired in an unsuccessful attempt to prevent a speech in Sligo by Arthur Griffith, the new president of the Free State.[15]

That same evening, Collins found himself in the middle of a shootout with antitreaty forces in Dublin. As he exited a motorcade, about a dozen armed men came piling out of a nearby house and rushed past him, firing at the cars. Instead of ducking for cover, Collins opted for a gunfight.

"Drawing my own revolver, I fired into them. I believe I wounded one," Collins said. "One lad discharged his revolver at me—he was only a few yards away—but fortunately he did not hit me." Collins chased the gunman into a doorway, disarmed him, and had him carted off to jail, then joked about the whole thing with reporters. "I asked him if he knew who I was, and when he said 'no,' I told him. That," Collins commented with a whimsical smile, "seemed to make him more uncomfortable than ever."[16]

It turned out that Collins was not the target—the gunmen were after the cars. But in the end, he might have been better off if the young rebel had managed to wing him—it would have taught the chairman of the provisional government of the Irish Free State the folly of trading potshots in the road.

With the IRA split, and half of it in open rebellion, the Free State needed a loyal defense force, so it began building a national army. In June, a new election for the Dail returned a large protreaty majority. On June 23, Dunne and O'Sullivan proved as good as their word, assassinating Field Marshal Wilson. They were arrested, convicted, and hanged after Pa Murray declined to go over to London to pull off a rescue. He said the mission was impractical, and besides, "After that American trip, I was not keen on taking up a job like that again."[17]

Whether the Wilson assassination was ordered by Collins or not—and there are some doubts—the outraged British blamed the hardline antitreaty faction holed up in the Four Courts. If Collins did not deal with the problem, the British Army would. On June 27, the antitreaty forces were given an ultimatum to surrender the Four Courts. When they ignored it, the National Army, with field guns borrowed from the British, opened an assault.[18]

The civil war was on.

In a repeat of the General Post Office in 1916, rebel resistance at the Four Courts collapsed after days of shelling. On the last day, an enormous explosion shook the complex—a store of explosives had been ignited, either accidentally by Free State artillery, or purposely by the rebels. The fighting spread throughout Dublin, and the nation, with the antitreaty side trying to hold the southern province of Munster.

Pa Murray, Dan Healy, and Martin Donovan all joined the antitreaty forces, along with much of the Cork IRA. Murray led a column to County Waterford, but when the Free State staged an amphibious landing at Passage West in Cork, behind rebel lines, Murray led another column in fighting there. With the antitreaty forces falling back, he moved to East Cork, and was briefly the second-in-command under Tom Barry there until he was appointed commander of the IRA in Great Britain in October.[19]

Murray was skeptical of the job from the moment the idea was mentioned. "Very little was done in England when everyone was with you," he wrote to a high-ranking IRA officer in September 1922, after the treaty split. "Now you have very few on your side—what do you propose to do?"[20]

After he took the job, he learned exactly what the IRA proposed to do—a major sabotage campaign in Britain, blowing up buildings and bridges. It was ridiculous, he said—like the Dunne rescue that he turned down the year before, it was so far beyond the realm of possibility that he never even considered it. Probably because he would have been the one blowing things up—in Britain, almost all key operations were handled personally by the "Officer Commanding, Britain," or a few close comrades. Despite the grandiose title, the commander didn't have much of a command.[21]

Instead of planting dynamite, Murray focused on providing logistical support for the boys back home. That meant arms and ammunition, and that meant contacting Soviet agents. The new rulers of the Kremlin had no more reason to love the Union Jack than the IRA did—just a few years before, Britain and the United States had tried to smother the Soviet Union in the cradle by sending troops to Murmansk and Archangel during the Russian Civil War.

The Soviet contacts yielded nothing immediately, but a seed had been planted. While it germinated, Murray and a few close associates went about buying guns and shipping them to Ireland.

Among those associates was Martin Donovan. In late July, after the civil war broke out, he was named a captain in the quartermaster's staff of the Cork city brigade. He took part in an ambush of National Army troops that wrecked a train at Tubereenmire, County Waterford, in September 1922. Later that month, Donovan was attached to the Great Britain Command under Murray, traveling to England to purchase arms and ammunition.[22] He was arrested on March 10, 1923, in Liverpool and deported to the Free State, where he was imprisoned until May 1923, when the civil war ended.

Healy, like Donovan, was supposed to be part of Murray's team in London. After returning from New York, he was attached to the headquarters of the Cork city brigade, taking dispatches to Limerick, Liverpool, and London. In September he was appointed commander of the 1st Battalion of the Cork No. 1 Brigade. Arrested that same month, he escaped from jail after two days, only to be captured again in November on his way to take over as adjutant of the Great Britain Command. Like Donovan, he languished in prison until the civil war ended in the spring of 1923 with the rebel forces routed and the National Army triumphant.

The fighting had lasted less than a year. The antitreaty forces had more combat veterans, but the National Army had more men, and artillery. De Valera finally acknowledged the reality with a proclamation to "Soldiers of the Republic, Legion of the Rearguard." He informed them: "The Republic can no longer be defended successfully by your arms. Further sacrifice of life would now be vain and continuance of the struggle in arms unwise in the national interest and prejudicial to the future of our cause."

The IRA hid its guns but never surrendered.

The civil war's most prominent casualty was none other than Michael Collins, who had authorized the New York attack on Cruxy. It happened when the big fellow returned to his native Cork, now an antitreaty hotbed. On August 22, 1922, he saw family and some old friends in West Cork—and he may have been planning to see a new enemy.

Eamon de Valera, it turns out, was nearby in a crossroads pub, at a conference of IRA commanders, including Pa Murray. When he learned of a plan to ambush Collins, de Valera tried to cancel the operation because he was there to meet Collins, an aide said, but the president of the Irish Republic was rebuffed by the IRA's commander, Liam Lynch.[23]

Late in the day—so late that most of the ambushers had departed— Collins's motorcade rounded a bend and ran up against the few who had remained. It was just a few hundred yards from the pub where Pa Murray and the other IRA officers had been meeting. As shots rang out, Emmett Dalton, a Free State general riding with Collins, ordered the driver to hit the gas and get out of there. Collins, up for a gunfight, countermanded the order.

In a repeat of that reckless Dublin shootout back in April, Collins leapt from the car with a rifle and returned fire at the attackers. At some point the weapon fell silent; he had been shot in the head. As the writer Frank

O'Connor put it with soaring eloquence: "The countryside that he had seen in dreams, the people he had loved, the tradition which had been his inspiration—they had risen in the falling light and struck him dead."[24]

It's never been definitively determined who fired the fatal shot. What is certain is the name of the place where it happened—the name had haunted Cork's rebels for six years: Beal na Blath.

It was the very spot where the Cork Volunteers got the message to stand down on Easter 1916. The shame of it had left such a bitter taste in the mouth of the messenger, Terence MacSwiney, that he starved himself to be rid of it. The shame of it had helped drive the Cork Volunteers to the vanguard of the fight for independence, and the fight against the treaty.

Now Beal na Blath would haunt an entire nation for a very different reason.

After the War: The Cork Crew

When the civil war ended, Murray, Donovan, and Healy, like de Valera, were left to carry on the struggle by other means. Murray returned to Dublin and was appointed adjutant general of the Irish Republican Army. Among his duties: Burying the corpse of the Irish Republican Brotherhood. The secret society, born on St. Patrick's Day in 1858, expired at age sixty-six, fatally weakened by the treaty split. In February of 1924, leaders of the antitreaty IRB voted to disband it. Murray was handed the task of conveying the news to the local branches, which he did at a meeting on November 2.[25] (The Free State faction of the brotherhood was wound down as well that year.)

Not long thereafter, the Soviet seed Murray had planted in London showed signs of sprouting.

In June 1925, Murray joined a delegation to the Soviet Union, where he met with Stalin himself in an effort to procure arms and pilot training from the Soviet air force for some Irishmen. The dictator got a kick out of Murray's grand title, Officer Commanding, Britain.[26] And decades later, Murray recounted that Stalin made clear in a half-hour one-on-one meeting that he was none too impressed with the art of rebellion as practiced in Ireland.

First, Murray claimed, Stalin produced a full list of weapons the Free State had seized from the IRA. If that caused Murray's jaw to drop, it probably hit the floor when Stalin informed him that members of the Irish delegation had been loose-lipped as they took a steamer to Hamburg, en route to the Soviet Union. Several people knew of the supposedly secret mission, Stalin said.[27]

Stalin had no confidence that any guns he gave to the rebels would remain in the hands of the IRA. He had no confidence that the operation could remain a secret from London. He had no confidence that Britain wouldn't invade the Soviet Union if the secret got out.

And besides, he told Murray, "Your revolution has not gone far enough."[28]

Exactly what that meant was made clear when a Soviet official asked another member of the IRA delegation, Gerry Boland, "How many bishops did you hang?"

"None," said Boland.

"Ah, you people are not serious at all."[29]

It all made for a great story, and later in life Murray was great for telling stories of his greatness. Maybe some of it even happened that way. In truth, the Soviets did not have a lot of guns to give away. They pointed out to the Irishmen that what they wanted could be found a lot closer to home: "Are there not plenty of arms in the Free State army? Cannot you train there?"[30] Besides, Ireland was a bit too far removed from the Soviet Union.[31]

No agreement was reached on weapons, but one question that Stalin asked Murray opened the way for future cooperation—could the IRA use its contacts in the Irish diaspora to aid the Kremlin?

The answer, either then or shortly thereafter, was yes. Though Murray would always deny involvement, a deal was worked out between the Kremlin and the IRA by the end of that year—money for information. Originally, the deal involved the IRA spying on Britain, but the espionage soon extended to the United States.[32]

And the main player in the American spying operation was none other than Pa Murray's old comrade from Cork, Sandow Donovan. The same man who led the Coolavokig ambush, and blamed Cruxy for its failure. The same man who ordered the poisoning of Cruxy.

"A true Irish James Bond," was how one account described Donovan.[33]

In 2001, Tom Mahon, an Irish researcher, stumbled across a stash of IRA documents from the 1920s that were written in code. He enlisted the help of a cryptographer, James J. Gillogly. Their work revealed a secret archive, and one of the most fascinating characters in it was "Mr. Jones," a pseudonym for a high-ranking rebel officer who was spying for the Soviets in America.

New York at the height of the Roaring Twenties was not exactly hardship duty, what with "swank hotels" and "good clothes," but the wry Mr. Jones made it sound that way. "My job is getting hard . . . wine and women," he wrote. "I am onto the right people now and can produce material of high order, but I have to bring good whiskey along and stay up all night drinking with whores and the people who give me the stuff."[34]

The material he forwarded to his Soviet handler, "Stephen," included reams of data on US chemical weapons, the blueprints for a Browning .50 caliber machine gun, technical information on airplane engines, and flight manuals from the Army's training school.

In return, the Soviets gave the IRA an estimated £500 a month; in 2022 that would be close to £34,000, or about $38,000. The secret army needed 80 percent of that just to stay in business.

When tension between the Soviet Union and Britain ratcheted up in late 1926 and 1927, Stephen approached Mr. Jones about the possibility of sabotaging British shipping in East Coast ports if war erupted.

By the time the Anglo-Soviet war scare blew over, both the IRA and Mr. Jones were getting a little tired of the Kremlin deal. The Soviets had temporarily turned off the money faucet, and Mr. Jones wanted to go to work for himself for a change.

Mr. Jones is a perfect match for Sandow Donovan. We know Jones was a highly placed IRA man, and there are indications his first name was Dan and that he was from Cork. His personality matched Sandow's—aggressive, and confident to the point of arrogance. And Donovan was in America during the period in question. He had to flee Ireland in March 1924, after he took part in an attack on British military personnel from a naval base in Cork that the British retained under the terms of the treaty. Dressed as Free State officers, Donovan and two other men opened up with a Lewis gun on a motor launch.[35] One British soldier was killed, and twenty-eight other people were wounded. Afterward, the attackers skedaddled to the New World under false names.

Sandow wasn't the only Irish republican ready to move on. De Valera, who had marched die-hard republicans into the political desert by abstaining from Free State politics, set his eye on greener pastures in 1926. He founded a new party, Fianna Fail (Soldiers of Destiny) that would sit in the Dail. Most of his followers joined him in a stampede toward the milk and honey of electoral politics.

By the end of 1926, Pa Murray had pretty much had it with the IRA, too.[36] On November 14, the organization launched dozens of attacks on the Free State police. Two officers were killed, and the ensuing government dragnet scooped up Murray and several other longtime Cork republicans. They knew the drill—it was laid out in IRA General Order #24. They were expected to deny the legitimacy of the Free State by refusing to recognize the court or cooperate in its proceedings.[37]

Instead, tired of what they saw as pointless bloodshed, they hired lawyers and asked for bail. They were done with the gunmen, and the gunmen were done with them. Murray moved to Dublin, and until he died in 1967, remained loyal to de Valera, who went on to lead the country in 1932, and for long decades thereafter. In his retirement, Murray would sit with de Valera in the park outside the presidential mansion, talking about old times.[38]

He also liked to spin stories for journalists. In 1964, Murray sat down with the journalist Tim Pat Coogan to recount his international adventures on behalf of the Irish Republican Army. He talked of stalking Balfour in Oxford, and of meeting Stalin in Moscow.

And then there was New York.

"What were you doing there?" asked Coogan. There was a moment's pause, in which Murray's eyes flickered, as though focused on something distasteful, Coogan wrote.

"Shootin' a poor divil," Murray said at last.

The old IRA man went on to weave a fantastic tale about the assignment to track down and kill O'Connor (a writer for the *New York Times* seems to have heard much the same story). In Murray's version, it was he who came up with a brainstorm for locating O'Connor, he who spotted the informer, and he who shot him:

"We'll find him at the Saint Patrick's Day Parade, for sure," Murray said he told his confederates. "He may be a bloody informer, but he's still an Irishman, isn't he?"[39]

By extraordinary luck, he told Coogan, O'Connor showed up right across the street from them at the parade.[40]

"It was all I could do trying to keep myself from crossing the street and putting my hands around his throat," Murray said. "I wanted to choke him to death, right there on the sidewalk."[41]

Instead, Murray claimed, he and his team enlisted the help of a sympathetic Irish American policeman to track O'Connor to his apartment at 583 Columbus Avenue. Then, about a month later, he shot O'Connor himself, with a gun borrowed from another New York policeman, he said.

"I was sorry after," he said with a sigh. "We heard later that the poor devil had been tortured to make him talk. We didn't know that at the time."[42]

Murray's self-aggrandizing stories are flatly contradicted by Dan Healy's detailed account to military historians. The Irish government found Healy's statement so convincing that, fearing he could face legal jeopardy, it redacted the part where he described shooting O'Connor.

There are so many wildly improbable parts to Murray's version—stumbling across the one man they were seeking among half a million at a parade, getting a police officer to stalk O'Connor for total strangers, having another policeman provide the gun—that his claims to be the mastermind, the spotter, and the triggerman feel like a fairy tale of New York. Could it be that an old man who played an active but largely unsung role in his nation's creation was just trying to cement a spot in history?

Martin Donovan certainly wouldn't contradict him—he had died decades before, in 1936 at age 48. A carpenter by trade, he kicked around through a few jobs after the civil war. Then, in 1933, the scourge of the Royal Irish Constabulary went to work as a policeman. And he wasn't pounding a beat as an unarmed Garda.

Donovan joined a newly formed special unit with a definite political bent. Dubbed "Broy's Harriers" for the police commander Eamon Broy, the unit would later harass the IRA, but it initially targeted the Blueshirts, a right-wing movement with fascist trappings. In 1933, the Blueshirts were planning a march on Dublin, and de Valera, who had come into power in 1932, did not like the sound of that. He recruited a lot of former IRA men as detectives for Broy's Harriers—they lacked police training, but they did know how to use the guns they were issued.

That experience came in handy on December 23, 1933, when Detective Donovan was assaulted by a gang of marching Blueshirts in Clonakilty, Cork. The trouble began when a heckler yelled "Up the Republic" and "Up Dev." Some Blueshirts expressed their displeasure in a manner befitting Italy's Blackshirts or Germany's Brownshirts. They started beating the daylights out of the guy. When Donovan and another detective moved to protect him, the Blueshirts turned on them with clubs.[43]

After taking a few whacks to the head, Donovan pulled his gun.

"Were you going to plug anybody?" a lawyer for an accused Blueshirt later asked in court.

"No, I was never going to do that," Donovan replied. Ever the calm one in the center of the storm, he simply made the arrest.

A month after his testimony, he was promoted to detective-sergeant and transferred to Mill Street Barracks in Cork city.[44] Two years later he died of lung cancer.

As Pa Murray and Dan Healy worked to ensure that Donovan's widow got a pension for his IRA service, former comrades heaped roses on his grave. "An outstanding man in the South," said Tom Crofts, a former IRA commander of Cork, adding that he was even better than the vaunted

Sandow Donovan.[45] Pa Murray called Donovan "unique," adding that no one gave better service in Cork city.[46]

"Martin was always recognized as being cool and courageous," Danny Healy told an Irish military historian in 1957. "Surely, he proved it to the full that night in New York, almost thirty-six years ago."[47]

But the mission that Martin Donovan took the greatest pride in was not the ambush at 84th Street—it was the MacNeilus prison break. Donovan kept a giant jail key that he carried away from the caper, carefully wrapped in oilcloth and hidden behind a brick that he cemented into place in the rear wall of his house in Cork. He called it the most valuable souvenir he owned.[48]

What no one dwelled on was Detective-Sergeant Donovan's role in killing policemen, or in the plan to assassinate the British cabinet. It would have been one of the worst terrorist assaults on a Western democratic government in modern history, but the two daring actions that Donovan and his friends preferred to recall were bloodless. They were ones in which the quiet gunman helped a comrade out of a tight spot with quick thinking and strong nerves.

In war stories, the blood is best forgotten.

Or at least redacted.

When in 2003 the Irish Military Archives released Dan Healy's statement recounting his days in the IRA, the bit about the gunfire in New York was omitted. The reason cited: "Would or might cause distress or danger to living persons on the grounds that they contain information about individuals or would or might be likely to lead to an action for damages for defamation." (That danger having passed, the archives released the redacted material to this writer in 2018.)

After the civil war, Healy worked as a clerk for the South Cork County Board of Public Assistance and Board of Public Health. He married, and raised a family on his modest salary.[49] He was a small, quiet man, deeply respected by the community—if he walked into a crowded pub, men would invariably stand to offer him a seat.

Unlike Pa Murray, Healy didn't like to talk about the war, and when he did speak of it, it was in humorous tales of getting spooked while trying to sleep in a graveyard. He was unashamed of his wartime deeds, but pained by them, nonetheless. He once told a grandson: "In the future you will learn things about me that will shock you, and I hope it won't change your opinion of me."[50]

When Healy died in 1983, his days in the old IRA qualified him for military honors at his funeral, but he had made clear to his family that he'd have none of that. Instead, his coffin was simply draped with the flag for which he had fought so hard: the Irish tricolor of green, white, and orange.

The Spies and the Fixer

Florrie and Jo O'Donoghue lived out their lives in the shadows cast by the civil war. They took neither side, and while Florrie adamantly opposed the treaty, he even more adamantly opposed a civil war. O'Donoghue resigned from the IRA leadership in June 1922 and worked thereafter to reconcile the protreaty and antitreaty forces and reunify the IRA. To that end, O'Donoghue met with Michael Collins shortly before he was killed at Beal na Blath. Collins's death only added to the bitterness of the civil war, but O'Donoghue kept at it, to no avail.[51]

Like Pa Murray, he went with de Valera in the 1926 split from the IRA, joining the new party, Fianna Fail. Like Danny Healy, he took a civil service job in Cork, as a tax collector for the county. When World War II broke out, he joined the Irish Army as an intelligence officer. Among his duties for a neutral nation: helping to catch Nazi agents and clamping down on American spy networks.

After the war, O'Donoghue went back to collecting taxes, and something more: war stories from the fight for independence. He convinced de Valera to set up the Bureau of Military History, which interviewed veterans, transcribed their recollections, and archived them.[52] Danny Healy and Pa Murray were among those who contributed. The book you are reading would not have been possible without that work.

O'Donoghue also wrote a glowing 1954 biography of Liam Lynch, the leader of the antitreaty forces during the civil war. And more than three decades after the fact, O'Donoghue was still concealing his wife's role as a spy in Victoria Barracks. "Cork No. 1 Brigade had established a most valuable contact at British 6th Division Headquarters, a lady who has not been persuaded to abandon the anonymity of the pseudonym 'G' under which she operated," he wrote in the biography, *No Other Law*.[53]

Perhaps Florrie's caginess should come as no surprise. As Sandow Donovan once said, "The O'Donoghues were, and I suppose are, the most secretive family ever born."[54]

O'Donoghue died in 1967, a little over a year after his beloved Jo.

Long after his death, O'Donoghue's peacemaking and historical labors landed him at the center of a conspiracy theory about the death of Michael Collins. An eleven-point post-action report from the Cork IRA presented the ambush as a straightforward affair. Point eight reads: "I have since learned that Ml. Collins was shot dead during the engagement."[55] But theories about exactly how and why the big fellow came to be killed at Beal na Blath abound, fueled by the extraordinary fact of de Valera's presence in the area, and that of so many ranking IRA men at the crossroads village less than a mile from the ambush.

In a 2018 book, *The Great Cover-Up*, Gerard Murphy makes a largely circumstantial case that under the guise of a neutral negotiator, "O'Donoghue pulled Collins into the trap" at Beal na Blath, because O'Donoghue, a die-hard republican, considered Collins a traitor for signing the treaty.[56] In a 2020 sequel, *A Most Reliable Man*, Murphy argued that it was O'Donoghue who was the traitor, "in the pay of British military intelligence since 1911."[57] It remains to be seen if Murphy's planned third book on O'Donoghue will clarify matters. (He also suggests that Cruxy's influence with Sean O'Hegarty stemmed from the brigade commander's sexual attraction to him.)[58]

Florrie's nemesis, Captain Kelly, the British Army spymaster, lived a life of shame and glory following the army's withdrawal from his native Ireland. After countless close encounters with shell and shot in World War I and the Irish revolution, he seems to have had trouble adjusting to the languid pace of peacetime life.

In 1926 he was transferred to the Army reserves, and two years later was court-martialed on sixteen charges of fraud and misconduct for embezzling £300—worth about £19,500, or about $21,850 in 2022. He pled guilty to ten charges; the others were dismissed. Kelly was booted from the military, but the luck that carried him through Cork held up—he escaped prison.

When World War II erupted, Kelly was in Coventry, England, and found a line of work that suited his martial temperament—chief air raid warden for a sprawling defense plant three miles north of the city center, the Coventry Ordnance Works, which produced mountings for naval guns.

Kelly's skill, daring, and experience faced a brutal test on November 14, 1940, when waves of Nazi bombers obliterated the bulk of the city. About two-thirds of Coventry's structures were destroyed or damaged. Kelly spent hellish hours frantically working to save his factory, then led a group of volunteers into the teeth of the firestorm engulfing the city, helping municipal crews battle the flames. He emerged covered in grime and glory and was awarded the new George Medal for civilian valor.

The citation read:

His personal activities on the night of an intensive air raid were largely instrumental in saving his factory from destruction. He extinguished an incendiary bomb and immediately afterward took twelve volunteers to help the City Fire Service deal with a serious fire. They attended at another fire and on the way back helped to extricate the bodies of policemen who were trapped in debris left by high-explosive bombs. A large high-explosive bomb hit a workshop, but fire was avoided by prompt action under Kelly's guidance. Until five o'clock in the morning Kelly continued to give inspiring leadership to his men.[59]

The city was devastated—over five hundred were dead. And Kelly's newfound fame had some devastating personal consequences. About two weeks after he was awarded the George Medal, he was in court on a bigamy charge.

Kelly had abandoned his wife and six children in 1934, without bothering to provide support. Then he remarried in 1939, without bothering to get a divorce. This led to quite a bit of legal bother in 1941. Kelly pleaded guilty to bigamy, and again escaped a prison sentence, thanks to the intervention of a government minister. He was ordered to pay £2 a week in child support, but he did not pay it for long.

Kelly was dead within the year. Kidney stones did what the German empire, the Irish Republican Army, and the Luftwaffe couldn't. His family, in need of money, sold his military decorations, but held on to the George Medal. The man was a cad, but he was no coward, and if his family could get some cash for his courage, they certainly deserved it.

Across the Atlantic in New York, Jimmy McGee stayed true to the republican cause through the treaty split, the civil war, and the de Valera split. He acted as a treasurer for Clan na Gael, funneling money to the IRA into the 1930s. At the end of that decade, he moved to Long Island City, across the East River from Manhattan. But he didn't leave the gunrunning game until he died around 1940.

"He was very cozy with every person sent from Ireland to obtain guns for Republicans," one historian wrote. After all, there was a gun shop right across the street from his home.[60]

One weapon McGee did not send to Ireland, according to his daughter, was the revolver he'd given Pa Murray for the Cruxy ambush. After he died, McGee's son tried to send the pistol to a museum in Dublin, entrusting it (of course) to a Carmelite priest in New York. But the priest died before he could get the gun to Ireland, and those who found it in his room could not comprehend what a man of God was doing with a pistol, or the role it had played in the only authorized attack on American soil by the Irish Republican Army.[61]

They deep-sixed the thing in the East River.[62]

It was a fitting burial at sea, given what happened with the *East Side*: weapons halted on their way to Ireland, and a buddy of McGee dumping some of the incriminating ordnance into the depths of New York harbor, that dark and forbidding reservoir of sunken secrets.

In Cork, the six young men slain at Ballycannon are remembered in stone and in song, and in stories passed along Blarney Street, where so many of them lived. A monument to their memory was raised in Clogheen in 1945. A more recent ballad names the fallen, and lays the blame:

But curse that Cruxy Connors, treacherous turncoat and spy
Who sold away on that fateful day the Ballycannon Boys.[63]

Chapter 14

▰▰▰

The Crux of the Matter

AGAINST ALL ODDS, Cruxy survived.

Any gambler would have had O'Connor near the top of their dead pool after the IRA fingered him as the villain of Ballycannon. But even with four bullet holes in him, O'Connor clung to life with all the determination of a man dangling from a windowsill.

And he wasn't giving anything away. The bullet to the jaw made it impossible to talk, but whenever he was asked who had shot him, his only response was a shake of the head. The spy who had stopped spying and the gunman who had stopped shooting was now the informer who wouldn't inform.

"O'Connor is said to know at least one of the three men who attacked him, but has never opened his mouth about it," the *Evening World* reported.[1]

By early June, it was clear that O'Connor would live. Slowly recovering in the hospital, he spent his days working a small weaving machine in his bed, under police guard. When he was well enough to move, O'Connor dragged his battered body across the border to Canada, a British dominion that was presumably safer than heavily Irish New York. He settled in Ontario, a few rail stops from Niagara Falls, staying as close as he dared to his New York family. And he could travel for free, thanks to his new line of work—as a special agent for the Canadian National Railroad Police.

He courted a fellow Irish immigrant, Claire, from County Leitrim, and they were married on Tuesday, November 25, 1924. On the marriage license, he gave England as his birthplace, but there's no doubt it was Cruxy—the license listed both his parents. The following spring, the family expanded with the birth of a daughter, Eileen. In February 1929, Claire and Eileen headed off to Scotland to visit her brother and sick mother in Glasgow. It was an extended stay—they remained until July 1930.

With his wife and daughter in Scotland, it appears that Cruxy went to stay with his parents at their apartment on Columbus Avenue in New York. When the 1930 census was taken, a man who identified himself as "Joseph O'Connor" was living with Cruxy's parents. Joseph was Cruxy's middle name, and this Joseph was the same age as Cruxy, and was married, but his wife wasn't present.

The census taker recorded O'Connor's occupation as "butcher." Maybe Cruxy had switched professions, yet again. Maybe the bullet to the jaw eight years earlier had affected his speech, so that when he said "bookkeeper" in his Cork brogue, the census taker heard "butcher."

Or maybe he was thinking of Ballycannon.

It says much about Cruxy's bonds with his family that he would return to the very neighborhood where he'd been shot eight years before. By now there were ex-IRA men all over New York City, self-imposed exiles who had left Ireland after the antitreaty side lost the civil war. Pension records show that one of them, Michael Kenny of B Company, 9th Battalion, Cork No. 1 Brigade, lived at 142 West 82nd Street, barely two blocks from the O'Connor apartment. Whether for that or some other reason, Patrick, Claire, and Eileen O'Connor settled in Brooklyn for a time when they were reunited after the Scottish sojourn.

It wasn't long before the family was again separated by the Atlantic. By the end of 1936, Cruxy, again using his middle name Joseph, had moved to Leigh-on-Sea in southeast England. In December of that year, he suffered shock and abrasions in a quintessential English crash—two double-decker buses colliding in the fog.[2] About a year later, in November 1937, Claire and Eileen joined him in Leigh-on-Sea after a journey from New York aboard the *President Roosevelt*.

The late 1930s were not a great time to move to Europe. When the British government conducted a special census in September 1939, just after World War II broke out, O'Connor was working as an auto salesman and spending his free time as a volunteer ambulance driver for the civil defense agency, Air Raid Precautions.

The Luftwaffe kept him busy.

The area around Leigh-on-Sea, like other coastal communities in southeast England, suffered frequent attacks from Nazi fighter bombers. A visitor in March 1943 recalled the scene: "Many shops were closed and boarded up, and there was much evidence of bomb damage. The London Hotel at the corner of Tylers Avenue was in ruins, and a number of shops including the jewelers R. A. Jones and their famous clock had suffered blast damage."[3]

During the war, auto sales went into a tailspin as manufacturers switched to the production of tanks and other military vehicles. So O'Connor added another profession to his lengthening resume—clock repair. After the war, he and Claire headed back to Canada, boarding the *Aquitania* out of South-ampton on March 10, 1947. They settled in Ontario, where their daughter got married three months after their arrival.

Cruxy died five years later, in 1952, at age sixty. Chiseled shamrocks adorn his tombstone.

The Why of It All

Buried with O'Connor was the motivation for the act that forever exiled him from his homeland. So let us try to unearth why he did what he did, with the full knowledge that the human heart can be the ultimate enigma.

Wars and revolutions may be fought over grand principles like indepen-dence or loyalty to the crown, but that's not to say that the people who fight those wars are always motivated by high ideals. Sometimes their actions are decided by self-preservation, personal agendas, and petty feuds. The Irish revolution was no exception. Charles McGuinness, an IRA officer from Derry, noted that "many a private grudge was satisfied under the guise of loyalty to Britain or Irish freedom."[4]

Revolutionary Cork offers any number of examples, but Jo Marchment is probably the best one. She cloaked her espionage as patriotism, but it was clearly a quid pro quo—she gave the IRA information so the IRA would kidnap her son from her hated in-laws in Wales. The transactional nature of her loyalties would certainly help explain some of the many peculiarities of her case.

A transaction can have dire consequences when one of the parties feels that they haven't been dealt with in good faith. By August of 1920, Jo had been helping the IRA for over a year, first in Youghal, then in Cork city. And after a year, she was no closer to getting Reggie back. From Jo's viewpoint, this quid pro quo was all quid and no quo. As Florrie put it, she "became doubtful of our intentions."[5]

She was determined to rectify the situation, and she was convinced that Terence MacSwiney held the key. So she scheduled a meeting with MacSwiney in city hall on the evening of August 12, 1920, to discuss the abduction of her child—an issue that had obsessed her for nearly two years, almost driven her to suicide, and led her to risk a treason charge and a firing squad. She said she was asked to write down all the facts and bring her statement to the meeting.

And then a number of very odd things happened.

First of all, she didn't show up for the meeting, and for the strangest of reasons. "I left home to get at the city hall at 8 o'clock" she said. "As I was leaving, my next-door neighbor called me and asked me to read the *Echo*. She was old and her eyesight was poor."[6]

So instead of heading off to her vital meeting with MacSwiney, she sat down with the old woman. Jo was so determined to get Reggie back that she would have other neighbors *killed*, but she was willing to skip a meeting on the subject with the lord mayor and the IRA's Cork commander so that she could read the newspaper to this neighbor?

While she didn't show up at city hall that night, her Victoria Barracks colleague Captain Kelly did, with scores of British troops, in an intelligence coup that scooped up Terence MacSwiney and nearly the entire leadership of the Cork IRA. Strangely, Jo's handler and lover, Florrie O'Donoghue, was not among those IRA leaders attending the meeting that night. And even stranger, all the IRA men but MacSwiney were released.

This is pure speculation but consider that if Jo had tipped off the British about the big IRA meeting, or merely learned at work of the impending raid, it would explain why she didn't go to city hall that night. And if she knew of the raid and didn't warn the republicans (other than, perhaps, Florrie), it would explain why she needed to come up with some excuse, however implausible, about why she didn't make it. But why would she tip off the British, or fail to warn the IRA?

Maybe she thought MacSwiney had qualms about the kidnapping. We know that while he led the Cork IRA, the project didn't move forward to Jo's satisfaction, and that once the British removed him from the scene, it did.

Florrie insisted the information that led to the city hall roundup came from an August 9 British raid on the mails and he was at pains to absolve anyone and everyone on his side: "There was not in the manner which this information fell into British hands any question of treachery, or even culpable negligence, on the part of anybody concerned."[7] Could it be that he was so touchy on the subject because he knew, suspected, or later learned that Jo had either instigated the raid or gotten wind of it and done nothing? After all, if the raid resulted from a letter intercepted on August 9, as Florrie insisted, Jo, the chief clerk in Kelly's office, would have had days to warn the IRA.

If Jo was working with both sides to advance her personal agenda, it would explain the bizarre yet undeniable fact that she was allowed to continue working in Victoria Barracks after it became known—indeed, highly publicized—that her son was kidnapped from Wales by Irish gunmen, and after it became clear that the IRA had a spy in Victoria Barracks sufficiently well-placed to set up intelligence officers for assassination, as Jo did with the three officers killed at Waterfall.

Liam Tobin, Michael Collins's right-hand man, marveled that the "suspicions which naturally the enemy would have toward her never materialized."[8] As late as May 1921, Jo was still leaking vital documents, and as late as May the British knew that vital documents were still being leaked, despite the firing of the suspected staff members. How could the British, even as a precautionary measure, not have suspended a woman whose son they knew had been abducted by Irish gunmen in a custody dispute?

Perhaps she was continuing to supply Captain Kelly with valuable information. The fact that he survived any number of IRA attempts to kill him is remarkable, and luck certainly played a role. But Kelly, a lady's man, always deftly sidestepped the sexual snares laid for him by his enemies, almost as if he'd been warned.

Was Jo callous and calculating enough to have a leg in both camps? Recall the fate of Frederick and James Blemens, whom she had had killed because of the amazing coincidence that two supposed British spies just happened to be close neighbors to an IRA spy. Their spy ring was reputedly based in the YMCA, but their names never turned up on the rolls of that organization, and though subjected to a prolonged interrogation, the pair never admitted to spying.

One theory is that Josephine had her neighbors eliminated not because she spotted suspicious meetings at their house, but because she didn't want them to spot suspicious meetings at *her* house.[9]

The neighborhood purge came from the same woman who made an office purge her first order of business as a spy—followed quickly by a charm offensive directed at the intelligence officers in Victoria Barracks, which presumably included Kelly.

And she so charmed another intelligence officer—Florrie O'Donoghue—that the top IRA intelligence officer in Cork married the daughter of a policeman, and the widow of a British soldier. If Jo was working both sides, that raises questions about how much Florrie knew about her activities.

It also raises questions about Kelly, because Britain was conducting a mole hunt in Victoria Barracks even as Jo was smuggling out secrets right and left. Might the womanizing Kelly have come to some understanding, pragmatic or romantic, with the beautiful, charming, and manipulative Jo Marchment? An understanding that either both would survive the deadly spy game in Cork, or neither would?

But was Kelly really such a cad that he would allow his colleagues to be killed, betraying the trust of the British Army to which he devoted his entire career? Recall that he ruined that career by betraying the trust of that army. Recall, too, how readily the womanizing Kelly committed an even more personal betrayal, abandoning his wife and six children without a farthing of support.

And it would not have been the first time that a crown official and an Irish rebel reached a pragmatic accommodation to keep each other alive. Superintendent John Mallon of the Dublin Metropolitan Police, the detective who cracked the Phoenix Park assassinations, tipped off the suspected mastermind of the killings, Patrick Egan, about his impending arrest, allowing him to flee. Egan had earlier scotched a plan to assassinate Mallon.[10]

Which is not to say that there is any concrete proof that Jo Marchment and Captain Kelly did something similar—the case is purely circumstantial.

But Jo wouldn't have been the only person in revolutionary Cork to use the IRA or crown forces to pursue their own agendas. If Felix O'Doherty's account is to be believed—and there is no reason to doubt it—the very appearance of the Ballycannon boys at the O'Keeffe farm on that fatal night stemmed from their interest in the killing of Long Con Sheehan as a suspected spy. And there are plenty of clues that Sheehan was set up for the killing by his landlady, with whom he had been feuding.

So let us consider how the question of self-interest applies to the central mystery of this tale: What motivated Cruxy?

There are two main theories about why Cruxy talked—the torture notion expounded by Pa Murray and others, and the idea that O'Connor was a spy all along, promoted by Sandow Donovan and others. Each has points in its favor, and drawbacks.

The accepted version among the IRA men who knew him best—the boys of C Company, like Pa Murray—was that O'Connor broke under torture, or at least a grueling interrogation. "He wasn't a spy at all," Sean Murray insisted. "I believe they gave him an awful gruelling, and this broke him down."[11]

As evidence, Sean Murray pointed out that O'Connor didn't identify Sandow Donovan or another IRA officer he knew, Michael Murphy, when the informer saw them imprisoned under false names in Victoria Barracks.

Jerry Deasy, whose family had feuded with the O'Connors for years, had no reason to be charitable toward Cruxy, but he bought the torture story.

"O'Connor was taken to military headquarters and probably tortured for info," Deasy wrote a family member. "He was a rather unstable, emotional type and, no doubt, could not take the treatment."

If only the IRA had a spy in Victoria Barracks who could tell us what happened in that interrogation room. Well, it turns out the rebels did have such a spy. Pat Margetts was a British soldier who was assigned to the detention quarters from January to May of 1921. He grew disgusted with the behavior of British forces in Ireland and started giving information to the IRA.

"Connors was in detention in a special cell," Margetts recalled. "On some excuse or another, I got up outside the cell. It was a process of kindness, this interrogation."[12]

A process of kindness.

Around 11 p.m. on the evening of Tuesday, March 22, 1922, it became clear that O'Connor was giving information, but Margetts said he couldn't get the word out to the IRA because he was on duty, and it was after curfew. All this transpired more than two days after O'Connor was taken into custody, and just hours before the Ballycannon raid. Had it occurred on Sunday or Monday, Margetts would have had time to warn the IRA.

"I talked to Connors myself," Margetts added. "He looked scared; anyhow, he had a furtive look in his eye and looked at you from under his eyelashes, but he had not been ill-treated, nor were there any marks on his face. I'd say that he would give information for money."

That would seem to drive a stake through the heart of the torture theory. But why would the men who knew O'Connor best seem so wedded to the idea? Perhaps because it not only absolved Cruxy to a certain degree, but them as well. They were the ones who vetted his membership in the IRA. They were the ones who would look like fools if they had admitted a British spy into their midst. Better to believe that a guy they grew up with was "a good chap, who got cold feet" at Coolavokig, as Sean Murray put it. Easier to sleep at night if the nightmare of Ballycannon was the result of bad luck and a spineless bookkeeper instead of a cold-blooded betrayal by one of their own—a lad from the neighborhood.

Such uniformity in the recollections of old comrades was not unusual in the annals of the Bureau of Military History. Some witness statements from Cork city were reviewed collectively by members of veterans' groups before they were submitted.[13]

And Pa Murray had a very personal reason for definitively declaring that Cruxy was tortured. Murray's mission was to kill the man, and that mission failed. Better to fail at killing the innocent than to fail at killing the guilty. Even a seemingly reliable narrator like Danny Healy had trouble with that failure—he resolved it by claiming that O'Connor had died of his wounds.

If the boys of C Company saw Cruxy as hapless and spineless, others, like Sandow Donovan, spun this portrait 180 degrees, turning O'Connor into a brave, battle-hardened, cunning foe. Sandow claimed the informer had been awarded the Croix de Guerre as a sergeant-major in the British Army.

He blamed O'Connor for everything that went wrong at the Coolavokig ambush, starting with alerting the British to the trap by dashing across the road, and ending with his failure to fire the machine gun. "We didn't know the reason then, but we knew later," Donovan said. "Cruxy was a spy for the British."

In this version, O'Connor never stopped serving the crown, from the Western Front to Coolavokig to Ballycannon. But while Sandow Donovan's story about O'Connor winning the Croix de Guerre in the British Army was repeated in some of the country boys' accounts of Coolavokig, we know it isn't true—his family says he never served in World War I. There's certainly no record that he did, and while many World War I personnel records were destroyed by Nazi bombing in World War II, military decorations like the Croix de Guerre were publicized in the London Gazette, and there's nothing in there about a Patrick O'Connor from Cork getting one. And none of the C Company men who discussed him—Pa Murray, Jerry Deasy, Sean Murray, and Danny Healy—ever said a word about him serving in the British Army, much less winning a medal. It's particularly striking that Sean Murray didn't, for he himself had served in the British Army.

Granted, there's a bit of circumstantial evidence to suggest that O'Connor might have been a spy all along. Things seemed to go wrong with machine guns whenever he was around. His Lewis gun did go silent at Coolavokig. And he was present at the raid on the Bowles farm in Clogheen, when the British confiscated another Lewis gun from the IRA, despite Mary Bowles's best efforts to conceal it. That raid came after a British soldier learned from his Irish girlfriend that the IRA was active in the area, but it was another source who pinpointed for British intelligence a house that was being used as an arms depot.[14] Could that source have been Cruxy, who knew the area like he knew his bedroom? Some people certainly believed so.[15]

And we could weave the O'Connor-Deasy feud into a-spy-all-along theory. The Bowles family was related to the Deasys. Could it be that Cruxy was merely pursuing his family's old vendetta with the Deasys and their relatives, using the authorities as a cat's-paw? If O'Connor's aim was to go after the

Deasys, it might explain a few things, like why he agreed to spy for the British in the first place—they had two sons in the IRA.

If O'Connor was a spy all along, his "capture" at church starts to look less like an unlucky arrest and more like an elaborate ruse to bring him in from the cold. Stan Barry, for one, was convinced that there was a "fake arrest made of him."[16] That would explain why his brother managed to get away, but Cruxy didn't, and why he chose to not use the gun he was holding, even though he knew civilians captured with arms could be executed. It would also explain why an RIC man intervened with the Auxiliaries to free P. J. Murphy, another IRA man caught in the church cordon—his arrest would just complicate a delicate operation.

But there's concrete evidence that casts strong doubt on the whole idea that O'Connor was a spy all along. An official report on the performance of the British Army during the Irish revolution made clear that while O'Connor was once a paid spy, he stopped reporting to his handler when he joined the IRA. It also says, tellingly, that while he talked, he didn't give it all away at once:

"A man who had been employed as an agent, but who had joined the IRA and ceased to give information, was arrested by RIC in Cork and found to be in possession of a revolver. He at once claimed to be a secret service agent. This man, after a very lengthy examination by a RIC officer and a military intelligence agent, gave away a great deal of information."[17]

Including the location of the Ballycannon safe house.

After the massacre there, the prisoner was "further interrogated and a great deal more useful information obtained," the report said. Had he been a paid agent, there would have been no reason for Cruxy not to spill everything he knew on Sunday, the day he was arrested. In fact, the Ballycannon boys would have been better off if he had—they weren't at the O'Keeffe farm at the time.

Instead, it took two days for O'Connor to give away Ballycannon, and even longer to give up the location of various arms dumps, where the British found rifles, revolvers, bombs, motorcars, a motorcycle, and ammunition. Whatever they confiscated, it wasn't everything—in the time it took for O'Connor to tell all, the IRA managed to spirit away a lot of its machinery.

And then there's the matter of Cruxy's failure to identify Sandow Donovan and Michael Murphy in the detention barracks. If he was acting as a paid spy, why wouldn't he point out some of the top IRA men in the city?

The tension between the two theories played out in Cork long years after the revolution ended.

When Ethel Cuthbert, the woman who impersonated Cruxy's mother to bring him a poisoned meal, applied for a pension for her service during the war for independence, several veteran leaders of the Cork IRA were appointed as a government advisory board for the case. They included Florrie O'Donoghue and Sean O'Hegarty, the former commander of Cork No. 1 Brigade who had led the Coolavokig ambush with Sandow Donovan. When the advisory board interviewed Cuthbert in 1945, she referred to O'Connor as a spy, which led to an interesting exchange:

Q. I do not think anyone ever suggested he was a spy.
A. He was a spy.
Q. He was shot all right?
A. Yes, he was a spy.[18]

It wasn't just his comrades from C Company who refused to believe that O'Connor was a spy all along. Some of the top leaders of the Cork IRA clearly felt the same way. But why would Sandow Donovan spread the notion that the man who wouldn't identify him was a paid spy all along, a daring and highly decorated veteran of World War I?

Perhaps because O'Connor frustrated Donovan at every turn, and it's better to be bested by an archvillain than a nervous bookkeeper. Cruxy's performance with the machine gun at Coolavokig ruined what could have been a glorious victory for the flying column Donovan commanded. When Cruxy spilled his guts and got six men killed at Ballycannon, he handed the Cork city IRA its worst single setback of the war. When Cruxy's mother broke free from the rebel squad detaining her, she spoiled Donovan's carefully constructed poison plot.

So, if Cruxy didn't talk because he was tortured, and didn't talk because he was a paid spy, why exactly did he talk? On one level, the answer is obvious—to save his life. But why did he give them some names, and not others? Recall that O'Connor identified not just the Ballycannon safe house, but three men—a British military communique about the raid said, "On information they were seeking three known murderers."

Thus, Cruxy was picking and choosing who he would give up. He didn't identify two IRA commanders whom he knew and who were using false names when he saw them at Victoria Barracks—Sandow Donovan and Michael Murphy. But he did give up the names of three men from C Company. It just so happens that two of the six C Company men killed at Ballycannon had served in the flying column with Cruxy—Willie Deasy and Jerry Mullane. As had Stan Barry.

A Theory

As one historian said of Khaki Cork's transformation into Rebel Cork, "driven by events, parties chose their ally of the moment, revealing an unexpected fluidity of loyalty." A more perfect description of Cruxy you could not find.

Here's a hypothesis on why he did what he did: Unnerved by Sinn Fein's challenge to Redmond's Irish Parliamentary Party, to which his family is likely allied, O'Connor offers to become a constabulary spy on the independence movement, which several members of the rival Deasy clan support. (Perhaps his feud with the Lee Road prostitutes plays a role as well.)

As the conflict heats up, O'Connor can no longer ignore the reality that the British are a bigger threat than the republicans. So, at some point he stops spying for the crown. Eventually, the pendulum swings even further, and he joins the IRA—as a true believer. Other Volunteers from the neighborhood vouch for him. He proves his bona fides by executing a spy in December 1920. He is considered so worthy that he is among the handpicked elite sent to join the brigade flying column in Ballyvourney, and is entrusted with a machine gun.

And that's when the wheels come off the cart.

It starts with the teasing. En route to Ballyvourney, O'Connor's comrades from C Company hang a mocking nickname on him, "Cruxy," because he mispronounces Croix de Guerre. He is an insecure, somewhat unstable man, so the teasing gets under his skin—all the more so because it comes from boys from his own neighborhood, several years younger than himself. Upstarts. And every single time that he hears the moniker, it stings anew.

On top of that, there are sidelong glances from the country boys in the flying column, suspicious because he likes to ask questions and jot down things in a notebook. There are snide comments about the christening he attended. Then comes the debacle at Coolavokig. When the Lewis gun jams, he comes under serious suspicion, and perhaps worse. Let's not forget the story that when he returned to Cork after the ambush, he had a black eye. If it came from a punishment beating by his own comrades from C Company, it would explain much of what followed.

O'Connor is arrested at church on a Sunday, and, after an intensive, sixty-hour interrogation, finally breaks down on Tuesday night. To save his life, he agrees to talk, but he only gives up those men he wants to give up, those who he feels deserve it—some of the C Company men who served with him in the column. They mocked him on the way to Coolavokig. They were out of position at Coolavokig. And they just may have beaten him after Coolavokig. Besides, his family had been feuding with Willie Deasy's family forever. So, he gives away the Ballycannon safe house, and names Deasy, Mullane, and perhaps Stan Barry, another C Company veteran of the flying column who didn't much like Cruxy, and was with the Ballycannon boys until the night they were killed.

For decades O'Connor's family had used the authorities to pursue their grudges. Perhaps he thought he was doing the same by betraying just three men—that was why he didn't give away the locations of the IRA arms depots right away. But he quickly discovered you can't betray a soldier without betraying the army and the cause he serves.

And so O'Connor had to be buried, along with the ugly truth of what motivated him. After all, it's bad enough to lose six men because someone gave up names under torture. It's worse if he gave up names because he was a paid spy all along, and the men he grew up and served with never realized it.

But what if he gave up those particular names not out of loyalty to the crown or pure greed, but because to stay alive he had to finger somebody, and he chose to sacrifice those comrades who made fun of him for going to a baptism and had a bit of craic about his bad French. What if the crux of the matter was the very nickname "Cruxy"?

Worst of all would be if six men died awful deaths for something so utterly petty.

Could such a slight really have been the snowflake that loosed an avalanche on the men at Ballycannon? Well, O'Connor wouldn't have been the first rebel in County Cork who flipped sides and avenged a slight in the first months of 1921. Just weeks before he talked, another IRA man, Dan Shields, turned informer after his comrades showed their disdain for him. He too, got six men killed.[19]

There is a ghost story they tell in that part of Cork about a farmer from Blarney who went out into his fields at night to count his cattle, and vexed by the fairies, became hopelessly lost, unable to find his way home. "So he turned his coat inside out, and he got out," the story concludes.[20]

In the days of old, Cork rebels were sometimes referred to as "the Fairies."[21] Of this we are sure: Cruxy, too, became hopelessly lost when, vexed by the rebels, he found that his familiar world in the fields beyond Blarney had suddenly turned unrecognizable. Like the farmer, O'Connor turned his coat. But he never found his way home. Instead, he spent the rest of his life wandering the wide world, from Ireland to England to New York to Canada and back again. Forever pursued by the relentless ghosts of Ballycannon.

ACKNOWLEDGMENTS

THIS BOOK WOULD not be possible without the contributions of many people, living and dead. Florence O'Donoghue, who is featured prominently in these pages, was instrumental in creating the Bureau of Military History, which collected stories from nearly 1,800 veterans of the War for Independence. Anything footnoted "BMH" stems from that work. Likewise, Ernie O'Malley, a leading IRA officer in the War for Independence and the Irish Civil War, collected interviews with about four hundred former rebel fighters. Any citation marked "O'Malley Notebooks" is the result of his labors. Both repositories proved to be gold mines in telling this story.

John Borgonovo, that beacon from University College Cork, lit the way into the Cork of a century ago with three works—*Florence and Josephine O'Donoghue's War of Independence* (Dublin: Irish Academic Press, 2006); *Spies, Informers and the "Anti-Sinn Fein Society": The Intelligence War in Cork City, 1919–1921* (Dublin: Irish Academic Press, 2007); and *The Dynamics of War and Revolution: Cork City, 1916–1918* (Cork: Cork University Press, 2013). John also steered me to the amazing story of Ethel Condon's attempt to poison Cruxy, as told in her pension application.

Andy Bielenberg of University College Cork provided a wealth of detail about deaths in the Irish War for Independence via his Cork Spy Files and kindly offered light to a stranger groping in the dark.

David Grant and his exhaustively researched website on the Auxiliary Division of the Royal Irish Constabulary, https://www.theauxiliaries.com/

index.html, were another valuable resource on many aspects of this story. David's thoughts on Cruxy were quite helpful.

Brian Hanley of Trinity College Dublin steered me away from any number of missteps and toward some pertinent material in reviewing the manuscript.

Tom Mahon, author of *The Ballycotton Job: An Incredible True Story of IRA Pirates* and coauthor of *Decoding the IRA*, and Gerry White, a local expert on Ballycannon, were generous with time and material. Tony McCarthy shared the ballad of the Ballycannon boys.

Breandán Mac Suibhne of the National University of Ireland, Galway, came to the rescue as I tried to decipher Ernie O'Malley's handwriting and the name for Cruxy O'Connor's Lewis gun, "Bás gan sagart" (death without a priest), providing a translation and the cultural context of the old curse. He also offered some helpful thoughts on the introduction.

The Deasy family kindly shared with me Jerry Deasy's written recollections of Cruxy O'Connor, along with the photo of Jerry and Willie Deasy that graces the cover of this book.

Claire Johnston, a graduate student in history at University College Dublin, helped me out in the midst of the COVID pandemic by digging up some pertinent interviews from the O'Malley Notebooks, and Gabrielle Brocklesby, a genealogy researcher, kindly consented to do the same for material in the Florence O'Donoghue Papers at the National Library of Ireland.

The above-named tried to help me get the story straight, and for that I am deeply grateful, but if I failed in any way, the responsibility is mine alone, not theirs. And if I have omitted anyone, I apologize—it was not through any malice aforethought.

NOTES

Introduction: Bloody Anniversaries

1. *New York Times* (hereafter *NYT*), April 20, 1921, 2, "Text of President Harding Speech to 'All Americas.'"

2. Ibid., "Ready to Fight for Monroe Doctrine."

3. Mariquita MacManus Mullan, "Unveiling Sally James Farnham's Bolivar—A Youthful Memoir," *Aristos* (Nov. 2007): https://www.aristos.org/aris-07/bolivar.htm, accessed Sept. 15, 2021.

4. *The Literary Digest*, April 209, 1922, 13, "New York's Big Foreign Population." There were 637,000 first- and second-generation Irish Americans in New York in 1920, far more than the 505,00 residents of all of Dublin County in 1926.

5. Seumas MacManus, *The Story of the Irish Race* (Old Greenwich, Conn.: Devin-Adair, 1975), 704.

6. Irish Military Archives, Bureau of Military History (hereafter BMH), Witness Statement 283, Seamus [sic] MacManus, 10. (Note: The pages cited are for the print version of material in the Bureau of Military History, so they are usually one higher than the digital page number, which accounts for the cover page.)

7. Ibid., 4.

8. BMH, Daniel Healy, Witness Statement (hereafter WS) 1656, 20.

1. The Ambush

1. *New York Herald* (hereafter *NYH*), April 14, 1922, 2, "Shot Fleeing Gang Near Central Park."

2. BMH, WS 1656, Daniel Healy, 20. Unless otherwise noted, this chapter's account of Healy's actions comes from his witness statement.

3. *NYT*, April 14, 1921, 2, "Link Shooting Here With Irish Warfare."

4. Irish Military Archives (hereafter IMA), Daniel Healy pension application, 12. Statement by Messrs. Corkery and Croft.

5. BMH, WS 814, Patrick G. Daly, 40.

6. *NYT*, March 17, 1972, 41, "The I.R.A. Connection."

7. *NYT*, April 14, 1922, 2, "Link Shooting Here With Irish Warfare."

8. Alfred J. Isacsson, *Always Faithful: The New York Carmelites, the Irish People and Their Freedom Movement* (Middletown, N.Y.: Vestigium Press, 2004), 87.

9. *NYT*, April 14, 1922, 2, "Link Shooting Here With Irish Warfare."

10. Ibid.

11. *NYH*, April 15, 1922, 12, "Victim of Sinn Fein Bullets Won't Talk."

2. Feuds and Fights

1. Stair na hÉireann/History of Ireland, "Clogheen Ambush | Six IRA Men From the 1st Battalion, Cork No. 1 Brigade Are Killed": https://stairnaheireann.net/2021/03/23/otd-in-1921-clogheen-ambush-six-ira-men-from-the-1st-battalion-cork-no-1-brigade-are-killed-when-they-are-surrounded-in-a-barn-in-clogheen-by-the-british-army-4/, accessed June 2, 2021.

2. Irish Census, County Cork, 1901.

3. *NYT*, Feb. 15, 1893, 2, "Acceptable to Irishmen."

4. *Cork Examiner* (hereafter *CE*), April 9, 1895, 6, "Blarney Petty Sessions—Yesterday."

5. Ibid., June 27, 1899, 8, "Blarney Petty Sessions—Monday."

6. Ibid., Dec. 3, 1908, 3, "Blarney Petty Sessions."

7. Ibid., March 11, 1899, 8, "Fatal Burning Accidents in the City."

8. Mary M. O'Leary, "The Waggetts of Kitsborough and some of the Houses and Families connected with them," Times Past, *Journal of Muskerry Local History Society*, 2010–11, Volume 9.

9. *CE*, April 28, 1903, 3, "Blarney Petty Sessions."

10. Ibid., Aug. 3, 1906, 8, "Blarney Petty Sessions."

11. Ibid., Sept. 8, 1911, 10, "Blarney Sessions."

12. John Borgonovo, *The Dynamics of War and Revolution: Cork City, 1916–1918* (Cork: Cork University Press, 2013), 59–60.

13. Ibid., 11.

14. *CE*, Aug. 20, 1904, 5, "The City Vacancy."

15. "The 1911 Railway Strikes," a lecture by Dr. Conor. McCade presented to the Irish Labour History Society, March 11, 2011: https://1913committee.ie/blog/?p=80, accessed Sept. 15, 2021.

16. Irish Census, County Cork, 1911.

17. Jeremiah O'Connor death notice, *Evening Echo*, Feb. 25, 1908, 4; John O'Connor death notice, *Evening Echo*, Dec. 5, 1911, 4.

18. Borgonovo, *Dynamics*, 7. In 1915, 288 Cork residents died of TB.

19. *CE*, July 4, 1910, 9, "Football."

20. *Irish Examiner*, Feb. 16, 2017, "On the quiet lanes and roads of Cork, road bowling is surviving in changed times": https://www.irishexaminer.com/sport/arid-20442988.html, accessed March 23, 2020.

21. *CE*, Sept. 18, 1914, 2, "Blarney Sessions"; March 17, 1916, 8, "Blarney Sessions"; May 30, 1916, 2, "Douglas Sessions"; Aug. 5, 1919, "Douglas Petty Sessions."

22. BMH, WS 869, P. J. Murphy, 1.

23. William Sheehan, *A Hard Local War: The British Army and the Guerrilla War in Cork 1919–1921* (Dublin: The History Press Ireland, 2017), 46–47.

24. Borgonovo, *Dynamics*, 8.

3. War and Rebellion

1. Borgonovo, *Dynamics*, 25.

2. *New-York Tribune*, Jan. 11, 1859, 6, "The Excitement in Ireland." (The article was datelined London, Dec. 24, 1858.)

3. Terry Golway, *Irish Rebel: John Devoy and American's Fight for Ireland's Freedom* (New York: St. Martin's Press, 1998), 37.

4. Borgonovo, *Dynamics*, 28.

5. IMA, Martin Donovan pension application, 28; Cork Census, 1911.

6. Borgonovo, *Dynamics*, 26.

7. Fearghal McGarry, *The Rising: Ireland: Easter 1916* (Oxford: Oxford University Press, 2016), 84.

8. BMH, WS 79, Diarmuid Donneabhain, 3.

9. Tom Mahon and James G. Gillogly, *Decoding the IRA* (Cork: Mercier Press, 2008), 159.

10. BMH, WS 1741, Michael V O'Donoghue, 50.

11. Mark Bulik, *The Sons of Molly Maguire: The Irish Roots of America's First Labor War* (New York: Fordham University Press, 2015), 26–27, 41–45, 53.

12. McGarry, 117.

13. Dorothy Macardle, *The Irish Republic* (Dublin: Irish Press Ltd., 1951), 169.

14. Piaras Beaslai, *Michael Collins and the Making of a New Ireland* (New York: Harper and Brothers, 1926), I:105.

15. "An American in Dublin," Mario R. Casey and Ed Shevlin, in *Ireland's Allies: America and the 1916 Easter Rising*, ed. Miriam Nyhan Grey (Dublin: University College Dublin Press, 2017), 310.

16. Dr. Mimi Cowan, "Irish-America and the 1916 Rising," Raidió Teilifís Éireann (Ireland's National Public Service Media; hereafter RTE): https://www.rte.ie/century ireland/index.php/articles/irish-america-and-the-1916-rising, accessed Sept. 21, 2021.

17. "Death on the Western Front during Easter Week, 1916," RTE: https://www.rte.ie /centuryireland/index.php/articles/death-on-the-western-front-during-easter-week-1916, accessed Sept. 21, 2021.

18. Macardle, *The Irish Republic*, 173–74.

19. Casey and Shevlin, *Ireland's Allies*, 311.

20. BMH, WS 79, Diarmuid Donneabhain, 4.

21. BMH, WS 1584, Patrick A. Murray, 4.

22. Borgonovo, *Dynamics*, 43.

23. BMH, WS 1656. Daniel Healy, 1–2.

24. Borgonovo, *Dynamics*, 91.

25. Bulik, *Sons of Molly Maguire*, 56, 173.

26. BMH, WS 1584, Patrick A Murray, 8.

27. Borgonovo, *Dynamics*, 86.

28. John Borgonovo, *Florence and Josephine O'Donoghue's War for Independence* (Dublin: Irish Academic Press, 2006), 30.

29. Ibid., 51–52.

30. University College Dublin Archives (hereafter UCDA), Ernie O'Malley Notebooks, P17/B-111, Raymond Kennedy, 83–84.

31. "Rescue of MacNeilus From Cork Prison," *Rebel Cork's Fighting Story: 1916–21* (Cork: Mercier Press, 2009), 40–42. Note: In Sean Daly's Witness Statement, based on a remembered conversation with Martin Donovan, the soldiers entered as the Volunteers were on the way out, not on the way in.

32. BMH, WS 1479, Sean Healy, 50.

33. Borgonovo, *O'Donoghue's War*, 52–53.

34. BMH, WS 1741, Michael V. O'Donoghue, 35–37.

35. Borgonovo, *O'Donoghue's War*, 53.

36. BMH, WS 1584, Patrick A. Murray, 10.

37. Ernie O'Malley, *On Another Man's Wound* (Dublin: Anvil Books, 1979), 109.

38. BMH, WS 838, Sean Moylan, 70–72.

39. BMH, WS 1644, Edward Horgan, 5.

40. IMA, Jeremiah Mullane compensation claim, Military Service Pensions Collection (two of two), 161, 183. Mullane was frequently referred to as Jerome.

41. IMA, Brigade Activity Reports, C Company, 1 Battalion, 1 Cork Brigade, 31.

42. David Grant, "The Auxiliary Division of the Royal Irish Constabulary": https://www.theauxiliaries.com/, accessed Sept. 26, 2021.

43. BMH, WS 1656, Daniel Healy, 6.

44. Ibid.

4. The Battle for Cork

1. IMA, Daniel Healy pension application, 13, Statement by Messrs. Corkery and Croft.

2. IMA, Martin Donovan pension application, 22, Statement by Patrick Murray.

3. Eunan O'Halpin and Daithi O Corrain, *The Dead of the Irish Revolution* (New Haven: Yale University Press, 2020), 125.

4. IMA, Martin Condon pension application, 10, Statement of Geo. Power.

5. BMH, WS 1584, Patrick A. Murray, 11–12.

6. On the use of chloroform during interrogations, see C. W. Muehlberger "Interrogation under Drug Influence," *Journal of Criminal Law and Criminology* 42, no. 4 (Nov.–Dec. 1951).

7. BMH, WS 1584, Patrick A. Murray, 11.

8. Peter Hart, *The I.R.A. and Its Enemies* (Oxford: Oxford University Press, 1998), 79.

9. Barry Keane, *Cork's Revolutionary Dead 1916–1923* (Cork: Mercier Press, 2017), 28.

10. BMH, WS 1584, Patrick A. Murray, 13.

11. BMH, WS 1656, Daniel Healy, 7.

12. Ibid.

13. BMH, WS 1584, Patrick A. Murray, 12.

14. Ibid., 14.

15. Borgonovo, *O'Donoghue's War*, 109n25.

16. BMH, WS 1584, Patrick A. Murray, 15.

17. BMH, WS 379, Jeremiah Mee, 10–12.

18. BMH, WS 1656, Daniel Healy, 10.

19. *Rebel Cork's Fighting Story*, 133.

20. BMH, WS 1413, Tadhg Kennedy, 34.

21. David Grant, "Campbell Joseph O'Connor Kelly, OBE, MC, MM": http://www
.bloodysunday.co.uk/castle-intelligence/kelly/kelly.html, accessed Oct. 1, 2021.

22. Peter Hart, *The I.R.A. and Its Enemies* (Oxford: Oxford University Press, 1998), 149.

23. BMH, WS 1584, Patrick A. Murray. 16–17.

24. Florence O'Donoghue, *No Other Law* (Dublin: Irish Press, 1954), 89.

25. Borgonovo, *O'Donoghue's War,* 127.

26. Hart, *The I.R.A. and Its Enemies,* 84.

27. *Freeman's Journal,* Aug. 17, 1920, 6, "Lord Mayor of Cork—Fateful Reply to Findings of Courtmartial."

5. The Doomsday Plot

1. Francis J. Costello, *Enduring the Most: The Life and Death of Terence MacSwiney* (Dingle, Ireland: Brandon Book Publishers, 1995), 22.

2. Ibid., 30–31.

3. Dr. Cathal Billings, *The Independent,* March 3, 2016, "Terence MacSwiney: Triumph of blood sacrifice": https://www.independent.ie/irish-news/1916/thinkers-talkers-doers /terence-macswiney-triumph-of-blood-sacrifice-34495537.html, accessed Sept. 25, 2021.

4. "Six things about the suffragette hunger strikes you should know," Museum of London: https://www.museumoflondon.org.uk/discover/six-things-you-didnt-know-about -suffragette-hunger-strikes, accessed Sept. 25, 2021.

5. Costello, 22.

6. Joe Doyle, "Striking for Ireland on the New York Docks," in *The New York Irish,* ed. Ronald H. Bayor and Timothy J. Meagher (Baltimore: The Johns Hopkins University Press, 1996), 361–62.

7. *Irish Echo,* March 14, 2012, "When New York Stopped for Terence MacSwiney": https://www.irishecho.com/2012/03/when-new-york-stopped-for-terence-macswiney/, accessed Sept. 25, 2021.

8. Doyle, *The New York Irish,* 364.

9. Ibid., 367.

10. *NYT,* Sept. 3, 1920, 1, "3,000 Strike Here to Humble Britain."

11. Doyle, *The New York Irish,* 357. Decades before, the Molly Maguire troubles in the hard-coal region of Pennsylvania began with a mine strike to protest Civil War conscription and ended with a mine strike to protest the mass hanging of Mollies. See Bulik, *The Sons of Molly Maguire,* 177–80, 283–84.

12. IMA, Pension Collection, James McGee pension application, 27.

13. *NYT,* Sept. 6, 1, "Premier Refuses Hylan's Appeal for Cork Mayor."

14. Costello, 170.

15. Shandon, *Rebel Cork's Fighting Story,* 35–36.

16. IMA, Brigade Activity Reports, C Company, 1 Battalion, 1 Cork Brigade, 23.

17. Nic Rigby, *BBC News,* "The Army general who charmed his IRA kidnappers," March 10, 2019: https://www.bbc.com/news/uk-england-beds-bucks-herts-46786760, accessed Sept. 26, 2021.

18. "British Army General Evades Capture by IRA": http://homepage.eircom.net/~cork county/strickland.html, accessed Sept. 26, 2021.

19. Costello, 150–51.

20. Ibid., 150.

21. BMH, WS 1584, Murray, 17–18.

22. Ibid.

23. Tim Pat Coogan, *Michael Collins: A Biography* (London: Arrow Books, 1991), 183–84.

24. IMA, Brigade Activity Reports, C Company, 1 Battalion, 1 Cork Brigade, 45.

25. BMH, WS 1479, Sean Healy, 48–49.

26. Ibid., 51.

27. Ibid., 51–52.

28. IMA, Martin Donovan pension application, statement by Patrick Murray, 22.

29. Dr. William Murphy, *RTE*, "Hunger Strike and Ireland, 1920": https://www.rte
.ie/centuryireland/index.php/articles/hunger-strike-and-ireland-1920, accessed Sept. 27,
2021.

30. *NYT*, Oct. 26, 1920, 1, "Mobbed at Meeting to Honor M'Swiney."

31. *New York Tribune*, Nov. 28, 1920, 1, "Catholics Make Protest Against Riot Over
Flag."

32. *Morning Star,* "The hunger strike that shook the British empire": https://morning
staronline.co.uk/article/f/hunger-strike-shook-british-empire, accessed Sept. 25, 2021.

33. Borgonovo, *O'Donoghue's War*, 141.

34. BMH, WS 1656, Healy, 11–12.

35. BMH WS 869, P. J. Murphy, 22.

36. Borgonovo, *O'Donoghue's War*, 142.

37. Grant, The Auxiliaries, "Cork Burning 11–12 December 1920": https://www.the
auxiliaries.com/INCIDENTS/cork-burning/cork-burning.html, accessed Sept. 23, 2021.

38. Gerry White and Brendan O'Shea, *The Burning of Cork* (Cork: Mercier Press,
2006), 110.

39. BMH, WS 1741, Michael V. O'Donoghue, Part 1, 98.

40. Borgonovo, *O'Donoghue's War*, 142.

41. UCDA, O'Malley Notebooks, P17–112, Mick O'Sullivan, 58.

42. Ibid., P17b-111, Stan Barry, 65–66.

43. Violet Peng, CBS, "The Magdalene Laundry": https://www.cbsnews.com/news/the
-magdalene-laundry/ accessed Sept. 27, 2021.

44. IMA, Brigade Activity Reports, C Company, 1 Battalion, 1 Cork Brigade, 43.

45. *Freeman's Journal*, May 25, 1921, 4, "Quarry Shooting." The identity of the
December quarry victim is unclear. P. J. Murphy, a member of C Company, recalled in
his Witness Statement that T. Sullivan, a former British soldier who lived on Blarney
Street, was "shot dead in [a] disused quarry on Lee Road," but his memory, decades after
the shooting, may have deceived him. A Christopher O'Sullivan of 132 Blarney Street was
executed by the IRA at Dennehy's Cross, on the south side of the Lee, six days after the
quarry shootings.

6. The Coolavokig Ambush

1. BMH, WS 1547, Michael Murphy, 30.

2. Ibid., 31.

3. IMA, Brigade Activity Reports, C Company, 1 Battalion, 1 Cork Brigade, 2.

4. BMH, WS 1547, Michael Murphy, 34–35.

5. Caoimh Mulvany, "The Parnell Bridge Ambush, Cork, 4 January 1921," The Irish
Story: https://www.theirishstory.com/2020/02/09/the-parnell-bridge-ambush-cork-4
-january-1921/#.YET3GZNKjIF, accessed Sept. 26, 2021.

6. BMH, WS 869, P. J. Murphy, 25.

7. *Evening Echo*, Aug. 30, 2008, 21, "The Pride of Sweet Clogheen."

8. *NYT*, April 15, 1921, 4, "Shot as a Traitor to Sinn Fein Army."

9. Dónal Ó hEalaithe, *Memoirs of an Old Warrior: Jamie Moynihan's Fight for Irish Freedom 1916–1923* (Cork: Mercier Press, 2014), 32.

10. Sean O'Callaghan, *Execution* (London: Muller, 1974), 124.

11. Author's discussion with a descendant, Sept. 14, 2019.

12. Patrick J. Twohig, *Green Tears for Hecuba* (Ballincollig: Tower, 1994), 179.

13. Information received by Dr. John Borgonovo, University College Cork, from a local source in Cork.

14. Mícheál Ó Súilleabháin, *Where Mountainy Men Have Sown* (Cork: Mercier, 1994), 105.

15. UCDA, O'Malley Notebooks, P17b-111, Stan Barry, 65.

16. UCDA, O'Malley Notebooks, P17b-112, Sean Murray, 31.

17. UCDA, O'Malley Notebooks, P17b-112, Mick O'Sullivan, 58.

18. UCDA, O'Malley Notebooks, P17b-112, Mick O'Sullivan, 58. I am indebted to Breandán Mac Suibhne for the translation and cultural context.

19. BMH, WS 878, Dr. Patrick O'Sullivan, 15.

20. Ó hEalaithe, *Memoirs of an Old Warrior*, 35.

21. BMH, WS 1543, Patrick J. Lynch, 15.

22. O'Callaghan, *Execution*, 120.

23. IMA, Patrick Murray pension application, 35.

24. O'Callaghan, *Execution*, 120.

25. BMH, WS 1532, Daniel Harrington, 13.

26. *Daily Mail*, Feb. 26, 1921, "Two Hours Battle With 400 Rebels."

27. UCDA, O'Malley Notebooks, P17b-112, Sean Murray, 33.

28. UCDA, O'Malley Notebooks, P17b-112, Mick O'Sullivan, 58.

29. Charlie Browne, *The Story of the 7th: A Concise History of the 7th Battalion, Cork No. 1 Brigade, Irish Republican Army from 1915 to 1921* (Schull: Schull Books, 2007), 57.

30. O'Callaghan, *Execution*, 122.

31. BMH, WS 1543, Patrick J. Lynch, 16.

32. BMS, WS 873, Charles Browne, 38.

33. "Activities of Ballingeary IRA 1920–1921": http://homepage.eircom.net/~sosul/page53.html, accessed Sept. 28, 2021.

34. UCDA, O'Malley Notebooks, Sean Murray, 33.

35. BMH, WS 878, Dr. Patrick O'Sullivan, 14.

36. BMS, WS 783, Michael O'Sullivan, 12.

37. O'Callaghan, *Execution*, 124.

38. UCDA, O'Malley Notebooks, P17B-111, Stan Barry, 62.

39. UCDA, O'Malley Notebooks, P17B-112, Mick O'Sullivan, 58.

40. O'Callaghan, *Execution*, 124.

41. IMA, Brigade Activity Reports, C Company, 1 Battalion, 1 Cork Brigade, 48.

42. BMH, WS 869, P. J. Murphy, 23.

43. Ibid., 27.

44. National Library of Ireland (hereafter NLI), Florence O'Donoghue Papers, Ms. 31,192, April 5, 1921, letter from adjutant general to O'Donoghue.

7. Bloodbath at Ballycannon

1. IMA, Brigade Activity Reports, C Company, 1 Battalion, 1 Cork Brigade, 12.
2. Andrew Bielenberg, University College Cork, Cork's War of Independence Fatality Register, Cornelius Sheehan: https://www.ucc.ie/en/theirishrevolution/collections/cork-fatality-register/register-index/1921-146/, accessed July 2, 2022.
3. *Freemans Journal* (hereafter *FJ*), Monday, March 21, 1921, 6, "Grim Cork Shooting."
4. Bielenberg: https://www.ucc.ie/en/theirishrevolution/collections/cork-fatality-register/register-index/1921-146/, accessed July 2, 2022.
5. *FJ*, Monday, March 21, 1921, 6, "Grim Cork Shooting."
6. Bielenberg: https://www.ucc.ie/en/theirishrevolution/collections/cork-fatality-register/register-index/1921-146/, accessed July 2, 2022.
7. BMH, WS 0739, Felix O'Doherty, 4.
8. *CE*, April 24, 1920, 8, "Tomas MacCurtain Memorial Fund."
9. Ibid., June 4, 1915, 17, "Blarney Sessions."
10. IMA, Brigade Activity Reports, C Company, 1 Battalion, 1 Cork Brigade, 24.
11. BMH, WS 1657, Daniel Healy, 12. Healy identified his companion in the pub shooting as "Jerome Mullane." It appears that Jeremiah Mullane and Jerome Mullane were the same person, because when Jerry Deasy identified Mullane's body, he signed an affidavit that he "knew and was well acquainted with Jerome Mullane of Blarney Street."
12. IMA, Pension Collection, Claim for Dependent's Allowance, Jeremiah Mullane (two of two), 161, 183.
13. IMA, Brigade Activity Reports, C Company, 1 Battalion, 1 Cork Brigade, 3.
14. BMH, WS 16, Riobard Langford, 3.
15. BMH, WS 1656, Daniel Healy, 8.
16. IMA, Pension Collection, Claim for Dependents Allowance, Michael O'Sullivan, 178.
17. BMH, Daniel Healy, WS 1656, sworn statement by Cornelius O'Keeffe, 1.
18. Ibid., 12.
19. Ibid., O'Keeffe statement, 1.
20. UCDA, O'Malley Notebooks, P17B-111, Stan Barry, 65. Also see BMS, WS 869, P. J. Murphy, 27, where Murphy says O'Connor "brought the Tans" to the farm.
21. BMH, Daniel Healy, WS 1656, sworn statement by Jeremiah O'Flaherty, 2.
22. Florence O'Donoghue, *No Other Law* (Dublin: Irish Press, 1954), 126, 144.
23. BMH, Daniel Healy, WS 1656, Statement by Morgan O'Flaherty.
24. *FJ*, March 24, 1921, 5, "Six Men Were Killed."
25. UCDA, O'Malley Notebooks, P17B-95, Stan Barry, 2.
26. Ibid., P17B-111, 65.
27. Ibid., P17B-95, 28.
28. *CE*, March 25, 1921, 5, "Clogheen Tragedy."
29. Beaslai, *Michael Collins*, II:203.
30. BMH, WS 1737, Seamus Fitzgerald, 29.
31. *Irish Independent,* March 28, 1921, 5, "Funeral of Cork Victims."
32. IMA, Pension Collection, Eily Murray pension application, 16.
33. UK National Archives, London, *Record of the Rebellion in Ireland in 1920–1921,* volume 2, 185.

8. A Basketful of Poison

1. IMA, Pension Collection, Ethel Cuthbert pension application, 145.
2. Ibid., 7.
3. BMH, WS 1706, Sean O'Connell, 4.
4. IMA, Cuthbert pension application, 124.
5. Ibid., 76.
6. Ibid., 127–28.
7. Ibid., 126.
8. Ibid., 146.
9. Ibid., 76.
10. UCDA, O'Malley Notebooks, P17B-112, Sean Murray, 31.
11. BMH, WS 1584, Patrick A. Murray, 21–22.
12. Ibid., 23–24.
13. Ibid., 24–25.
14. BMH, WS 1479, Sean Healy, 38–39.
15. UCDA, O'Malley Notebooks, P17B-112, Sean Murray, 32.
16. BMH, WS 1656, Daniel Healy, 15.

9. The Spying Game

1. Borgonovo, *O'Donoghue's War,* 110.
2. Ibid., 112.
3. Ibid., 113.
4. Everard Wyrall, *The Fiftieth Division: 1914–1919* (Uckield: Naval & Military Press, 2002), 240.
5. Borgonovo, *O'Donoghue's War,* 117.
6. Ibid., 118–19.
7. Michael Dame, *Mythical Ireland* (London: Thames and Hudson, 1996), 113–14.
8. Borgonovo, *O'Donoghue's War,* 11.
9. Ibid., 23.
10. Ibid., 25.
11. IMA, Pensions Collection, Florence O'Donoghue pension application, 69.
12. Borgonovo, *O'Donoghue's War,* 125.
13. IMA, Pensions Collection, Josephine O'Donoghue pension application, 34.
14. Ibid., 41.
15. Ibid., 40.
16. Ibid., 45.
17. Ibid., 38.
18. Ibid., 31.
19. John Borgonovo, *Spies, Informers and the 'Anti-Sinn Fein Society'* (Dublin: Irish Academic Press, 2007), 28–31, 171.
20. BMH, WS 1547 Michael Murphy, 33.
21. IMA, Pension Collection, "Kidnap and killing of James and Frederick Blemens": https://www.militaryarchives.ie/collections/online-collections/military-service-pensions -collection-1916-1923/brigade-activities/operation/kidnap-and-killing-of-james-and -frederick-blemens/, accessed June 22, 2021.

22. Borgonovo, *O'Donoghue's War*, 121, 126–27.
23. Ibid., 126.
24. Ibid., 130.
25. Ibid., 131, 137.
26. Ibid., 132–33.
27. Ibid., 134–35.
28. IMA, Josephine O'Donoghue pension application, 32.
29. O'Donoghue, *No Other Law*, 120.
30. IMA, Josephine O'Donoghue pension application, 32.

10. A Boatload of Tommy Guns

1. BMH, WS 1060, Seamus Finn, 43. It was actually more like five hundred guns, but it is unclear if it was Collins or Finn who was exaggerating.
2. UCDA, O'Malley Notebooks, P17B-108, Mick Leahy, 110.
3. BMH, WS 1056, Very Rev. Timothy J. Shanley, 6.
4. Sean Cronin, *The McGarrity Papers* (New York: Clan na Gael, 1972), 98.
5. Bill Yenne, *Tommy Gun: How General Thompson's Submachine Gun Wrote History* (New York: Thomas Dunne, 2009), 28.
6. Cronin, *McGarrity Papers*, 98.
7. Ibid., 28.
8. Yenne, *Tommy Gun*, 59–60.
9. Ibid., 61.
10. Tom Barry, *Guerrilla Days in Ireland* (Dublin: Anvil, 1989), 193.
11. Yenne, *Tommy Gun*, 60–61.
12. Cronin, Appendix VIII, 5.
13. BMH, WS 1056, Very Rev. T. J. Shanley, 3. The expletive was deleted in the original.
14. Peter Hart, *The IRA at War 1916–1923* (Oxford: Oxford University Press, 2003), 181.
15. BMH, WS 1056, Very Rev. T. J. Shanley, 1.
16. *NYT*, June 17, 1921, 2, "Seized Irish Guns Provide Mystery."
17. Ibid., June 20, 1922, front page, "Harvey's Son Held in Arms Plot."
18. Ibid., June 27, 2007, B1, "The End of an Era at Bellevue and a Nearby Church."
19. Robert Emmett Curran, "The McGlynn Affair and the Shaping of the New Conservatism in American Catholicism, 1886–1894," *The Catholic Historical Review* 66, no. 2 (1980):184–204.
20. *NYT*, June 27, 2007, B1.
21. Isacsson, *Always Faithful*, 4.
22. *NYT*, Aug. 31, 1937, 23, "Rev. P. E. Magennis of Carmelite Order; Prior General, 1919–32, Ex-Head of Friends of Irish Freedom, Dies in Dublin at 69."
23. Isacsson, *Always Faithful*, 80.
24. Ibid., 85.
25. BMH, WS 1056, Very Rev. T. J. Shanley, 6.
26. IMA, Pensions Collection, MA/MSPC/RO/606, New York Gun Running Participants, etc., 6.
27. Ibid., 13.
28. Ibid.
29. Ibid.

30. IMA, New York Gun Running Participants, 12.

31. Ibid., 7–8.

32. Ibid., 15.

33. *NYT*, June 17, 1921, 2, "Seized Irish Guns Provide Mystery."

34. BMH, Shanley, WS 1057, 1.

35. *NYT*, Sept. 7, 1960, 42, "Eugene Kinkead, Banker, 84, Dies."

36. BMH, WS 1057, Shanley, 1.

37. BMH, 1744, Sean Nunan, 15–16.

38. *NYT*, June 17, 1921, 2, "Seized Irish Guns Provide Mystery."

39. *New York Daily News*, June 18, 1921, 4, "All U.S. Crime Forces Seeking Gun 'Runners.'"

40. *The Independent*, Nov. 29, 2019, "The Clontarf home of IRA rebel Traynor is up for sale": https://www.independent.ie/life/home-garden/homes/the-clontarf-home-of-ira-rebel-traynor-is-up-for-sale-38735695.html, accessed Sept. 29, 2021.

41. IMA, New York Gun Running Participants, 10.

42. *NYT*, Sept. 27, 1921, front page, "One Arrest Here in Irish Gun Plot."

43. *NYT*, June 20, 1922, front page, "Harvey's Son-in-Law Held in Arms Plot."

44. Yenne, *Tommy Gun*, 64.

45. Karen Blumenthal, *Tommy: The Gun That Changed America* (New York: Roaring Brook, 2015), 58.

46. *NYT*, June 20, 1922, front page.

47. Hart, *The I.R.A. at War*, 190–91.

11. Passages

1. US National Archives (hereafter USNA), publication numbers M237 and T715, New York Passenger List and Arrivals, Names and Descriptions of British Passengers Embarked at the Port of Liverpool, July 30, 1921, *Carmania* of the Cunard Line.

2. Colin Simpson (London: Weidenfeld and Nicolson, 1977)

3. USNA, List or Manifest of Alien Passengers for the United States Immigration Officer at Port of Arrival, New York, *Carmania*, Aug. 8, 1921.

4. BMH, WS 1656, Daniel Healy, 15.

5. Ibid., 17.

6. Beaslai, *Michael Collins*, II:274.

7. Ibid., 276.

8. BMH, WS 1656, Healy, 16.

9. Borgonovo, *O'Donoghue's War*, 83.

10. Ibid.

11. Julie Kavanagh, *The Irish Assassins* (New York: Atlantic Monthly Press, 2021), 154.

12. Proceedings of the Old Bailey: https://www.oldbaileyonline.org/browse.jsp?id=t18831119-75-offence-1&div=t18831119-75, accessed Sept. 28, 2021.

13. Bulik, *Sons of Molly Maguire*, 159–62.

14. Ibid., 309–10.

15. Wayne G. Broehl Jr., *The Molly Maguires* (Cambridge: Harvard University Press, 1964), 153.

16. Arthur Conan Doyle, *The Complete Sherlock Holmes* (New York: Doubleday, 1930), Vol. II, 1,152.

17. BMH, WS 1656, Healy, 18.

12. The Hunt

1. National Museum of American History, "The Connected City": https://american history.si.edu/america-on-the-move/connected-city, accessed Sept. 29, 2021.

2. *The Literary Digest*, April 29, 1922, 13, "New York's Big Foreign Population."

3. BMH, WS 1656, Healy, 17.

4. Ibid., 18.

5. Golway, *Irish Rebel*, 258.

6. Michael Doorley, "Judge Cohalan and American Involvement in the Easter Rising," *Ireland's Allies*, 161–62.

7. BMH, WS 913, Shanley, 1.

8. Ibid., 1–2.

9. *NYT*, Nov. 13, 1946, 25, "Daniel F. Cohalan, Ex-Justice, 81, Dies."

10. Cronin, *The McGarrity Papers*, 76.

11. BMH, WS 587, Edmund O'Brien, 54.

12. Cronin, *McGarrity Papers*, 17.

13. Golway, *Irish Rebel*, 277.

14. Ibid., 278.

15. Cronin, *McGarrity Papers*, 84–85.

16. IMA, Pension Collection, James McGee pension application, 29.

17. BMH, WS 1744, Sean Nunan, 14.

18. BMH, WS 587, Edmund O'Brien, 46.

19. Ibid., 46–47.

20. Ibid., 50–51.

21. Ibid., 56.

22. Ibid., 58.

23. UCDA, O'Malley Notebooks, P17B-108, Mick Leahy, 110.

24. IMA, Pensions Collection, Patrick Murray pension application, 39.

25. BMH, WS 1656, Healy, 18–19.

13. The Heel of the Hunt

1. Isacsson, *Always Faithful*, 88.

2. *NYT*, Dec. 6, 1959, 86, "Owen Bohan Dies; Ex-Judge Was 78."

3. Central Park Conservancy Magazine, "The Story of Seneca Village": https://www.centralparknyc.org/articles/seneca-village, accessed Sept. 30, 2021.

4. *NYT*, Nov. 23, 1924, Section XX, 3, "Plunkitt, Champion of 'Honest Graft.'"

5. Isacsson, *Always Faithful*, 88.

6. BMH, WS 1656, Daniel Healy, 21–22.

7. Ibid., 22.

8. Ibid., 23.

9. UCDA, O'Malley Notebooks, P17B-89, Patrick Murray, 61.

10. *NYT*, April 15, 1922, front page, "Irish Rebels Seize Dublin Four Courts."

11. Macardle, *The Irish Republic*, 589.

12. Beaslai, *Michael Collins*, II:321.

13. Frank O'Connor, *The Big Fellow* (Dublin: Poolbeg, 1997), 78.

14. Macardle, *The Irish Republic*, 611.

15. *NYT*, April 17, 1922, front page, "Shooting at Sligo Fails to Prevent Griffith Meeting."

16. *NYT,* April 18, 1922. front page, "Collins Repulses Twelve Assassins and Captures One."

17. IMA, Murray pension application, 39.

18. Macardle, *The Irish Republic,* 744.

19. IMA, Murray pension application, 23.

20. Hart, *The I.R.A. at War,* 163.

21. Tom Mahon and James Gillogly, *Decoding the IRA* (Cork: Mercier, 2008), 159–60.

22. IMA, Martin Donovan pension application, 8, 23.

23. Coogan, *Michael Collins,* 407.

24. O'Connor, *The Big Fellow,* 213.

25. John O'Beirne-Ranelagh, "The IRB from the Treaty to 1924," *Irish Historical Studies* 20, no. 77 (1976): 38.

26. Emmett O'Connor, *Reds and the Green: Ireland, Russia and the Communist Internationals 1919–1943* (Dublin: University College Dublin Press, 2004), 112.

27. Coogan, *The IRA,* 72.

28. Mahon and Gillogly, *Decoding the IRA,* 249.

29. Coogan, *The IRA,* 72.

30. Uinseann MacEoin, *The I.R.A. in the Twilight Years: 1923–1948* (Dublin: Argenta, 1997), 643.

31. O'Connor, *Reds and the Green,* 112.

32. Mahon and Gillogly, *Decoding the IRA,* 250.

33. Ibid., 273. Sandow was also a bit of a Blackbeard, with a starring role in the antitreaty IRA's 1922 seizure of a British munitions ship. See Tom Mahon's *The Ballycotton Job: An Incredible True Story of IRA Pirates* (Cork: Mercier Press, 2022)

34. Ibid., 264.

35. MacEoin, *The I.R.A. in the Twilight Years,* 100–1.

36. Ibid., 116.

37. Mahon and Gillogly, *Decoding the IRA,* 108.

38. MacEoin, *The I.R.A. in the Twilight Years,* 116.

39. *NYT,* March 17, 1972, 41, "The I.R.A. Connection."

40. Coogan, *The IRA,* 73–74.

41. *NYT,* March 17, 1972, 41, "The IRA Connection."

42. Coogan, *The IRA,* 74.

43. *Southern Star,* April 21, 1934, 6, "Clonakilty District Court."

44. *CE,* May 10, 1934, 12, "Detective's Promotion."

45. IMA, Martin Donovan pension application, 10.

46. Ibid., 26.

47. BMH, WS 1656, Daniel Healy, 23.

48. BMH, WS 1479, Sean Daly, 50.

49. IMA, Daniel Healy pension application, 38.

50. Email from a descendant, April 13, 2022.

51. Borgonovo, *O'Donoghue's War,* 198, 201–2.

52. Ibid., 207.

53. O'Donoghue, *No Other Law,* 120.

54. IMA, Agnes McCarthy pension application (she was Florrie O'Donoghue's sister), 41.

55. Brian Hanley, *The IRA: A Documentary History 1916–2005* (Dublin: Gill & Macmillan, 2010), 48–50.

56. Murphy, *The Great Cover-Up,* 142.

57. Gerard Murphy, *A Most Reliable Man* (KDP Publications, 2020), 207.

58. Ibid., 170–72.

59. David Grant, "Campbell Joseph O'Connor Kelly, OBE, MC, MM": http://www .bloodysunday.co.uk/regimental-intelligence/kelly/kelly.html, accessed June 16, 2021.

60. Isacsson, *Always Faithful,* 87.

61. In 1994, two New York City residents—John Millar, a former member of the Provisional Irish Republican Army, and the Rev. Patrick Moloney, an Irish-born priest— were convicted on charges related to the daring robbery of $7.4 million from a Brinks depot in Rochester, N.Y., the year before. The bulk of the money was never recovered, and there was speculation that it went to the Irish republican cause. But no proof ever emerged that the IRA had any role in the crime, much less authorized it, and the judge in the case ruled that the IRA could not be mentioned at the trials. See Gary Craig's *Seven Million: A Cop, a Priest, a Soldier for the IRA, and the Still-Unsolved Rochester Brink's Heist* (Lebanon, N.H.: University Press of New England, 2017).

62. Ibid., 88.

63. *Evening Echo,* Cork, Saturday, March 24, 2007, 21. The ballad was written by Bert Ahern.

14. The Crux of the Matter

1. *The Evening World* (New York), June 8, 1922, 12, "Ex-Irish Soldier Guarded by Police Slowly Recovers."

2. *The Luton New and Bedfordshire Advertiser,* Dec. 10, 1936, 13, "Double-Decker Buses Locked in Fog Crash."

3. BBC, "A Day at the Seaside," Nov. 21, 2005: https://www.bbc.co.uk/history/ww2 peopleswar/stories/37/a7154237.shtml, accessed Oct. 1, 2021.

4. Charles McGuinness, *Sailor of Fortune,* Chapter 13, "A Peep in Ireland": http:// www.cmcguinness.net/, accessed Sept. 28, 2021.

5. Borgonovo, *O'Donoghue's War,* 126.

6. Ibid., 121.

7. O'Donoghue, *No Other Law,* 89.

8. IMA, Josephine O'Donoghue pension application, 33.

9. Murphy, *The Year of Disappearances,* 114.

10. Kavanagh, *The Irish Assassins,* 241–43.

11. UCDA, O'Malley Notebooks, P17B-112, Sean Murray 31.

12. Ernie O'Malley, *The Men Will Talk to Me: Galway Interviews* (Cork: Mercier, 2013), 280–81.

13. Eve Morrison, "Witnessing the Republic: The Ernie O'Malley Notebook Interviews and the Bureau of Military History Compared," in *Modern Ireland and Revolution* (Newbridge: Irish Academic Press, 2016), 138.

14. Sheehan, 87–88.

15. O'Callaghan, 124.

16. UCDA, O'Malley Notebooks, P17B-95, Stan Barry, 27.

17. *Record of the Rebellion in Ireland,* Vol. II, 185.

18. IMA, Ethel Cuthbert pension application, 126–27.

19. Hart, *The IRA and Its Enemies*, 149.

20. University College Dublin, National Folklore Collection, The Schools' Collection, Volume 0349, 005, "A Ghost Story": https://www.duchas.ie/en/cbes/4921722/4893663/5182844, accessed Oct. 1, 2021.

21. George Bennett, *History of Bandon* (Cork, 1869), 419: "A lot of the disaffected in this kingdom banded themselves together—as Fairies, Redboys, Whiteboys, Levellers."

INDEX

Mark Bulik is a senior editor at the *New York Times*. He is the author of *The Sons of Molly Maguire: The Irish Roots of America's First Labor War.*

EMPIRE STATE EDITIONS SELECT TITLES FROM EMPIRE STATE EDITIONS

Colin Davey with Thomas A. Lesser, *The American Museum of Natural History and How It Got That Way*. Forewords by Neil deGrasse Tyson and Kermit Roosevelt III

Mike Jaccarino, *America's Last Great Newspaper War: The Death of Print in a Two-Tabloid Town*

Angel Garcia, *The Kingdom Began in Puerto Rico: Neil Connolly's Priesthood in the South Bronx*

Jim Mackin, *Notable New Yorkers of Manhattan's Upper West Side: Bloomingdale–Morningside Heights*

Matthew Spady, *The Neighborhood Manhattan Forgot: Audubon Park and the Families Who Shaped It*

Robert O. Binnewies, *Palisades: 100,000 Acres in 100 Years*

Marilyn S. Greenwald and Yun Li, *Eunice Hunton Carter: A Lifelong Fight for Social Justice*

Jeffrey A. Kroessler, *Sunnyside Gardens: Planning and Preservation in a Historic Garden Suburb*

Elizabeth Macaulay-Lewis, *Antiquity in Gotham: The Ancient Architecture of New York City*

Ron Howell, *King Al: How Sharpton Took the Throne*

Phil Rosenzweig, *Reginald Rose and the Journey of "12 Angry Men"*

Jean Arrington with Cynthia S. LaValle, *From Factories to Palaces: Architect Charles B. J. Snyder and the New York City Public Schools*. Foreword by Peg Breen

Boukary Sawadogo, *Africans in Harlem: An Untold New York Story*

Alvin Eng, *Our Laundry, Our Town: My Chinese American Life from Flushing to the Downtown Stage and Beyond*

Stephanie Azzarone, *Heaven on the Hudson: Mansions, Monuments, and Marvels of Riverside Park*

Ron Goldberg, *Boy with the Bullhorn: A Memoir and History of ACT UP New York*. Foreword by Dan Barry

Peter Quinn, *Cross Bronx: A Writing Life*. Foreword by Dan Barry

Jill Jonnes, *South Bronx Rising: The Rise, Fall, and Resurrection of an American City, Third Edition*. Foreword by Nilka Martell

Matt Dallos, *In the Adirondacks: Dispatches from the Largest Park in the Lower 48*

Brandon Dean Lamson, *Caged: A Teacher's Journey Through Rikers, or How I Beheaded the Minotaur*

For a complete list, visit www.fordhampress.com/empire-state-editions.